NO STRINGS ATTACHED:
The Story of The Jonah Project

This book is dedicated to each and every person and child who was brave enough to reach out for help, all those who have found healing and those still fighting for their freedom. May this offering breathe life into your stories.

A special thanks to the church families, school counselors, donors, law enforcement agents, and our brothers and sisters who fight for freedom alongside us. If your name is not mentioned in these pages – it is solely because of your safety or because I cannot possibly include all of you by name.

The investments in all those you've touched as part of The Project; the rolled up sleeves and scuffed shoes from the work you put in, the risks you took – they will never be forgotten.

...and to my wife and the advocates who carry the torch now.

TABLE OF CONTENTS

Passage 1 — Riding the Wind	8
Passage 2 — Would You?	10
Passage 3 — A Pair o' Cleats	12
Passage 4 — Compassion Is a Basic Need	17
Passage 5 — No Leverage	20
Passage 6 — She Asked for Coach	23
Passage 7 — What Love Requires	25
Passage 8 — When No One Names It	28
Passage 9 — The Critical Figure	32
Passage 10 — Relocation Was Refuge	35
Passage 11 — The Best Ability Is Availability	41
Passage 12 — Aftercare Was the Point	45
Passage 13 — A Place at the Table	49
Passage 14 — Diamond in the Snow	53
Passage 15 — Learning to Be Free	57
Passage 16 — Crossing the Bridge	60
Passage 17 — Lighthouse	62
Passage 18 — City Hall	65
Passage 19 — Kids Saving Kids	68
Passage 20 — Freedom Railroad	71
Passage 21 — An Offering in the Sun	74
Passage 22 — The Business of Ministry	76
Passage 23 — A Mother's Plea	79
Passage 24 — When It Doesn't Get Easier	82
Passage 25 — Seeds Planted…	85
Passage 26 — The Great Equalizer	89
Passage 27 — Ordinary Miracles	93
Passage 28 — Staying	96
Passage 29 — Lessons	100
Passage 30 — When Jonah Becomes a Memory	102
An Open Letter from the Author	105
Testimonies & Appendix (Jonah Manual)	108

Preface

It might make sense to begin any story about human trafficking—the brutal reality of humans selling other humans—by rattling off statistics.

Statistics like these:
The average age a child is pulled into this nightmare is twelve.
One in four homeless teens will be trafficked in their lifetime.

It's also the fastest-growing criminal enterprise in the world.
There are more slaves on earth today than at any point in history.
Ever.

But the number that has haunted me most is this one:

Seven years.

That's the average life expectancy of a child caught up in "the life."

Seven years.

It becomes a clock you carry in your head and your heart—after every rescue, every relocation, every connection with a new victim. How much time do we have left before we lose them forever?

Numbers can inform you.
They can even alarm you.

But they can also numb you to what needs to be done.

And they don't begin to scratch the surface of how bad the reality actually is—how much grooming goes on, how much risk our kids face every single day, often right in front of us.

For those of us who have touched this work—felt its weight, its life—Jonah's story is about far more than statistics or tragedy.

It's rooted in something my family and I had been wrestling with long before we ever knew what human trafficking looked like up close. Somewhere deep inside—between our souls and the hearts we had given to Jesus—we were asking a simple but unsettling question:

What should our response be to a God who loves us without condition?

A Savior who seeks us out wherever we are—who comes for us no matter how deep the darkness, no matter the cost?

You'll see, I hope, that this is less a story about slavery than it *is a story about freedom*—our birthright as daughters and sons of God.

Yes, the Jonah Project became focused on anti-trafficking. And if I can say it plainly, we've been loudly proclaiming a freedom movement for more than a decade now. We've welcomed hundreds into the fight. Perhaps by the time this story is finished, it will be thousands.

I hope so.

The problem is that many worldly enterprises—programs, institutions, even churches—require something in return for their service or love. Sobriety. Program completion. Bible studies. Baptism. Discipleship classes. Attendance.

The offer of love comes with a catch.

It often demands more than Christ requires, while offering less than His freely given promise of living water.

In other words, it comes with strings.

But what if we challenged each other to cut them?

What does it look like to love like Jesus—or as close as we can come—regardless of how impractical it seems, how risky it feels, or how badly it fits existing service models?

Can we trust God to show up?
To heal the hurting and give wisdom to the helper?
To place resources in the right hands at the right time?
To place people in the right places at the right time?

Can we believe that the goodness of God is powerful enough to change lives without ever leveraging a single soul?

What if the answer to all of those questions is *yes*?

What would that kind of love look like?

To be fair, the Jonah Project is not one story at all—it's many lives intertwined, tuned to the call of freedom. It's the choice to love. The choice to be light. The choice to believe again—or perhaps for the very first time—that love still wins.

Even when you feel powerless in the face of overwhelming darkness.

This is a story of churches rallying together. Of homes opened. Of school kids engaging their world. Of victims becoming advocates. It's a story about what it means to walk with someone—not just for a moment, but for the long road after they've been to hell and back.

To see the light return to their eyes.
To witness resurrection in real time.

The Jonah Project was a radical experiment.

And it worked.

It still is.

Not because of the righteousness of the cause or the tenacity of the people involved—but because God never stops seeking. He still saves the lost. Still comes for us when we cry out to Him.

Without condition.
Without strings.
No matter what.

Passage 1 - Riding the Wind

I wasn't looking to start a ministry. I was just trying to stay faithful.

In 2014, I was serving as a part-time, unpaid pastor and working as an assistant baseball coach at a local high school in Spokane. My days were full—coaching, helping neighbors fix broken things, running a couple of free baseball clinics, and raising our sons, alongside my wife, Bindi. We had also taken in a young man named Tom as well, who we call Tommy Boy. He called me Papa Bear. His mom had passed, and he had nowhere else to go. So we brought him in. Our finances were threadbare, but our hearts were full. I was spiritually on fire—grateful, alive, and deeply in love with what Jesus was doing in my family. He had saved our marriage, filled our home with long-needed peace, and somehow—even in scarcity—He kept providing.

At the time, I didn't even know what human trafficking was.

Looking back, I realize I'd been around it before—I just didn't know what to call it. Gang prostitution was common in the neighborhoods I grew up in: first in the East Bay of California, then in northeast Albuquerque, and a few other rough patches in between. My parents struggled to hold jobs, and stability was something we never had for long. By fourteen, I'd left home and was eventually adopted by some relatives back in San Jose, where I attended San Jose High School and graduated in 1994.

A year earlier, I'd met the love of my life as she walked down the staircase from the school library—a girl named Bindi. She's now my wife.

Bindi and our two boys moved to the Washington–Idaho area in early 2008, searching for a safer and more hopeful upbringing than either of us had known. I joined them at the end of that year, and eventually we settled in the greater Spokane area, living in a small home up in the mountains with our horses and a wolf dog.

At that time, I wasn't a believer. Bindi was raised in a Hindu household, and our marriage had its fair share of hard chapters. But somehow, we held together. Then one day—out of my most desperate cry—I met Jesus in the middle of a wheat field in Greenbluff, Washington. No flashing lights. No church stage. Literally blinded by light, tears streaming down my face... it was like, there He was- telling me He'd always been there. Always would be. Calling me son.

One of the first things He impressed on me was how unconditionally He loved me—and how far He'd go to prove it. I would and still do, often hear His voice in the shower, in dreams, in quiet whispers—Little by little, He has reshaped my life.

Each morning, Jesus was usually the first thing on my mind. I'd wake up with gratitude and a deep sense of belonging I'd never felt before. That peace began to create in me a bit better husband, a more present father, and a man more capable of love..

So I started offering what I had.

Sometimes it was helping a friend paint his house or lay sod. Other times it was taking Tommy Boy and our skateboards downtown, carrying sandwiches made from dollar-store peanut butter and jelly, and sitting with the folks who slept in tents under the freeway.

My sons joined in too—raking leaves for an elderly couple down the street, which somehow turned into our Wednesday morning tea and Bible study. Me, three teenage boys, and this couple we'd just met.

It was wherever I felt Jesus leading. It was riding the wind. It was honest

Passage 2 - Would You?

I'd been coaching my son's Little League team—just doing what I always did. Teaching the game. Connecting with kids. Being loud, animated, and completely in my zone.

What I didn't know was that my best friend Tony—who worked as a custodian at the junior high—was inside the building nearby and happened to hear me.

He told me later he stopped in his tracks and thought, *That sounds like Aaron.*

He watched for a bit, out of view, and never said a word. But later that night, I got a text from him. It read:

"I saw you coaching today. It was awesome. I've never seen you more alive and in your element, and you were really getting through to those kids."

Tony and I joke around all the time. He's not usually the guy who drops serious encouragement out of nowhere. But that text stuck with me. It lit something in me.

Not long after, I reached out to volunteer at Rogers High School. I already had a connection there—I had coached their head football coach's son—and soon they offered me an assistant coaching role.

But there was a catch.

I'd already been coaching for a few years. I had experience. People told me I was good at it. But this role meant coaching under a brand-new, twenty-one-year-old head coach. I'd be taking direction from someone half my age with almost no experience.

At first, it felt beneath me.

So I went to God about it. I sat quietly and asked Him what I should do.

I heard a question.

Would you?

At first, I thought He meant: *Would you just obey? Would you humble yourself?*

But then I realized He was asking something deeper.

Would you have the conversation with Me?
Would you still include Me in your decisions?
Or are you back to making moves and expecting Me to ride in the sidecar?

So I sat with it.

Would I?

Would I hang out with kids, teach them baseball, and stay open to whatever God wanted to do—in their lives and in mine?

You're darn right I would!

Passage 3 — A Pair o' Cleats

Paraclete*: from the Greek paraklētos — one called to stand beside another; an advocate, helper, and comforter who speaks for the soul when it cannot speak for itself.*

I was around Rogers High most afternoons because of baseball. My sons played, and that gave me another reason to be present—not just as a pastor or a volunteer, but as a dad. Over time, a few of the students who didn't play started hanging around to watch the games. Maybe it was curiosity. Maybe it was something more.

Our church family would come out too—cheering for the boys, supporting the team. It wasn't official, but it started to feel like community.

One afternoon, I was helping a kid warm up to pitch. I looked down and saw he was standing on the mound in black socks.

"Charlie, get your cleats on, dude—you're going in to pitch."

He looked back at me and said, "I don't have any, Coach."

"Well then put your shoes on, brother—but you're pitching today."

"I don't have any shoes either."

I started to say something, but Coach Chris leaned in quietly and said, "Hey Coach—he's not lying. He doesn't have any shoes."

The world is often looking for grand miracles. This one wasn't grand. It was about trusting God to do something with whatever you had to offer.

In my case, it was the last twenty-six dollars in my family's bank account.

So we went to Ross and bought that kid—with size fifteen feet, by the way—a pair of cleats.

Later that week, a school counselor named Ryan emailed me to say thank you. Not for the shoes. For noticing. For caring. That was the moment something shifted.

I looked around Spokane and saw programs everywhere—nonprofits, agencies, churches. More than five hundred churches. Many doing good work, all trying to meet basic needs. And I kept asking myself, *Why me? Why would God call a man with no money, no title, no experience, to step into something this big?*

The answer came quietly.

Because you know I am enough.

I didn't have a plan and couldn't possibly meet all the needs I was seeing.

What I did have was a growing conviction that God wanted me to figure out how to offer compassion—and cut the strings.

Rogers High sat on the east side of Spokane, but to me it might as well have been another version of east San Jose or northeast Albuquerque—underfunded, overlooked, and full of stories nobody was asking to hear.

That's where I met Ryan Douse..

He walked like a man on a mission—long strides, always moving a little too fast for the hallway traffic—and smiled like he knew something you didn't. Kids gravitated to him. Athletes, kids skipping class, kids barely hanging on. When Ryan passed through a crowd, it parted. Not because he demanded it—but because he saw them.

That was rare.

Ryan was sharp, compassionate, and deeply committed to making a system work for kids it was never built to serve. He'd heard I helped one of the boys on my team get a pair of cleats and reached out to say thanks. That's how it started.

We talked. First emails. Then face-to-face. No strategy sessions. No vision casting. Just honesty. We were seeing the same thing: kids slipping through cracks so wide you could drive a truck through them.

Ryan didn't happen to be a Christian. But he opened a door most people never would've considered. He invited me—a pastor—to walk the halls of a public high school.

No preaching No altar calls.
Just presence and availability.

And that was the first miracle.

Not long after, a young woman who is like a sister to me, Liberty Allen and I, were invited to sit down with school administration. The athletic director sat across from us—calm, steady.

After we talked through the very few resources we actually had, she told us a story.

One winter night around eleven-thirty, a boy knocked on the gym doors. It was close to twenty degrees. He had nowhere else to go.

The janitor saw him. She wanted to help—but district policy said she couldn't open the door. Liability.

So she called the police.

The police took the boy home. Back to a father who was drunk, high, and angry. The same man who had kicked him out.

The A.D. didn't say what happened next. She didn't have to.

I reached for a sticky note.

I wrote my number and slid it across the table.

"If there's ever a kid in trouble," I said, "call me. Doesn't matter where they are or what time it is. I'll go get them. And I'll bring them back to you safely in time for first period."

She looked at me for a long moment, then nodded.

That little yellow square of paper didn't look like much.

But it was enough.

I didn't know it then, but that was the real day the Jonah Project began.

After that meeting, I spent more time on campus—sitting in Ryan's classes, walking halls, being available. Nothing formal. Just space. And every so often, a kid would talk. Not because they were told to. Because it felt safe.

One day Ryan invited me to coffee. Around the table were an English teacher, a YMCA director, a Young Life leader, and a few others. Men already in the trenches. Not churchy. Not performative. Just people who cared.

The same truth kept surfacing: housing.

At the time, Spokane estimated over 1,500 homeless teens. And I'd learned a statistic that stopped me cold—one in four would be trafficked at some point in their life.

The conversation drifted toward a big vision. Dorm-style facilities. Centralized care. Wraparound services. All good. All probably needed.

I asked a different question.

"What about the kid sleeping in a car tonight?"

That's usually where conversations get uncomfortable.

Because the solution moves from someday to now. From funding to inconvenience. From vision to your spare bedroom.

What if people opened their homes? What if we housed a kid this week, not someday?

That's where the difference often lived—not in belief, but in approach.

Most people want to help. They just want it organized. Safe. Manageable.

But we'd rather plan for the future than disrupt our present.

Even among allies, the fires that burned in our hearts burned in different places.

And that tension—between vision and immediacy—was often its own battleground.

Passage 4 — Compassion is a Basic Need

Before Jonah had a name, before trafficking entered our vocabulary, and before rescue or advocacy became part of our lives, there was a small church in the Garland District.

I was pastoring there at the time. I had no seminary degree—just a calling that felt like another miracle of grace for my family. God had placed us in a community where our hearts could flourish and where we would form deep, lasting friendships. It was a gift.

Much of my time was spent with the kids.

We'd meet in the church basement and talk. Real conversations. Honest questions. Or we'd head down to Clark Park during normal church activities and sit together, talking as a group. Nothing dramatic. Nothing staged. Just time spent together.

The pastor and his wife were beyond supportive. They believed in me, in my family, and in the small, early work God was doing—even when it didn't yet have a name or direction. They became important to much of Jonah's earliest formation, long before we understood what the work would become.

Looking back, this is where the root took shape.

Not in a strategy session.
Not in a crisis.
But in a church body learning how to love practically and locally.

It was out of this community that our first advocates emerged. At that point, I hadn't been called into fighting slavery. We were simply learning how to care for kids. I began asking church families, couples, and community members across town to "sponsor" a student at Rogers High.

The idea was simple.

I'd seen $50 a month advertised everywhere for sponsoring international kids. So I thought—why not offer the chance to sponsor a local child in need?

That $50 usually went first toward a GSL card—a card students needed in order to participate in school events and sports. They cost about $40. The remaining $10 from the first month often went toward taking the kid out for a burger and fries.

By the second month, it might be shoes.
Or help with a utility bill.
Or something else entirely.

It wasn't a program. It was responsive.

I remember one young man in particular. A counselor warned me he might not accept help. Said he was guarded. Unwilling. I was advised not to push.

So I didn't.

Instead, I leaned into humility. I told him how terrible I was with style and fashion. I asked if he'd come with me to the mall to help me pick out shoes—for another student. I told him I'd buy him Burger King if he helped me out.

He agreed.

By the time we reached the mall, his guard had lowered a bit. By the time we were in the Vans store, I could feel trust starting to form.

I looked at him and said, "Hey—why don't you grab a pair too?"

And he did.

No pitch.
No charity moment.
No explanation.

Just dignity, offered sideways.

That season taught me something essential: **help doesn't have to announce itself to be holy.**

We weren't fighting slavery yet. We didn't know how dark the road ahead would be. We were simply learning how to show up without leverage—how to meet needs without triggering shame, and how to preserve agency even in the act of giving.

The work didn't start with chains.

It started with burgers.
With shoes.

Passage 5 — No Leverage

The first place Jonah made an impact was not in how to relocate or "rescue."
It was how to show up without an agenda.

Before there were phone calls in the middle of the night, before there were emergency placements or conversations about trafficking, there was something much smaller and much quieter. There was the practice of noticing. Of responding to what was right in front of us without trying to turn it into anything else.

Small acts of care don't change a life on their own.
But they can change what someone believes about the world.

At the time, none of it felt like the beginning of anything. It felt ordinary. Necessary. The kind of thing most people would do if they were paying attention. But what it created was something rare: help without leverage. No expectation of gratitude. No requirement to attend church. No pressure to explain why the need existed. Just dignity offered without a hook.

Trust grows there.

It grew slowly at first—through presence in hallways, conversations with students, relationships with school staff who were carrying far more than their job descriptions allowed. Doors opened not because Jonah had a program, but because it didn't. Because there was no pitch. Just availability.

Soon, kids began reaching out. Sometimes for serious help. Sometimes just to talk. Counselors began calling, not because there was a policy to follow, but because they had nowhere else to turn. The trust wasn't built through expertise; it was built through consistency. Through answering when others didn't. Through staying when things got uncomfortable.

What became clear very quickly was this: people who have been exploited are experts at spotting strings.

They know when help comes with expectations attached. They recognize when kindness is conditional, when support is transactional, when love is being offered in exchange for compliance or gratitude or spiritual performance. Many had already lived inside systems where survival depended on giving something back.

So Jonah learned to remove the hooks.

Needs were met without requiring stories. Help was offered without demanding change. Presence came before process. And because of that, people stayed long enough to be seen. Long enough to be honest. Long enough for deeper needs to surface.

That kind of trust doesn't scale easily.
It can't be forced.
And it can't be rushed.

But it changes everything.

As relationships deepened, the realities underneath them became harder to ignore. Exploitation between kids. Grooming through phones. Adults profiting from chaos that looked, from the outside, like bad choices. What started as kindness became clarity. What began as presence became responsibility.

But none of that would have been possible without the first lesson being learned fully: trust is not built through solutions. It's built through restraint.

You don't earn trust by fixing people.
You earn it by refusing to use their pain as leverage.

Looking back, it's tempting to see those early moments as obvious steps toward something larger. They weren't. They were simply responses to what was right in front of us. Conversations. Rides. A willingness to walk this out without knowing where it would lead.

But that posture—kindness without leverage—became the foundation everything else rested on. Without it, rescue would have failed. Aftercare would have collapsed. Advocacy would have sounded hollow.

Trust came first.
Everything else followed.

Passage 6 - She Asked for Coach

I didn't know her. Not really.

I'd probably seen her around campus in passing, but I didn't remember her face—and she didn't know much about me either. So when one of the school counselors said a student had asked to speak with *Coach Tilbury*, it caught everyone off guard. Including me. Apparently she was one of the kiddos that was hanging around when I'd taken the baseball team for Dairy Queen.

The girl's name was Tabitha, but the kids called her Tabi. She'd been meeting with a counselor for other personal things—emotional things, hard family things. Nobody expected her to reach out to a pastor, let alone one she didn't know. But that's how desperate they were to get her some help.

So I showed up.

I walked into that room not knowing what I was walking into. And the truth is, it was awkward. I could feel it. Tabi sat quietly, looking down, and I was just some bald, bearded, tattooed guy sitting across from her—a total stranger who somehow was supposed to help.

I noticed a couple of counselors watching through the window. They didn't know me yet. I probably looked more like security than ministry.

But something in me knew I had to earn this girl's trust.

Not with words.
Not with Bible verses.
Just by being there—and letting her speak when she was ready.

And she was.

Within five minutes, she opened up and told me what was going on—what was happening to her younger sister.

Tabi told me something that changed me forever.

She said a pimp who was hurting her sister went to her school. He was actually in her math class. When the teacher wasn't looking, he would lean in close and whisper, *"You're next."*

It hit like a punch to the gut. Not just because of what she said—but because of how normal it seemed to her. Like this was just how life worked. Like this was the hand they'd been dealt.

I didn't know what to say. I didn't know what I could do.

But I knew God was present in that room. And that knowledge was the only thing that kept me grounded.

Later that afternoon I boarded the yellow school bus, alongside the Head Coach and a bunch of rowdy dudes, headed for our Junior Varsity Baseball game. Coach could tell something was going on with me, and he asked me about it. I was stuck - and I can't remember what I stuttered in response.

My mind was in another place.

This was no longer about cleats and utility bills.

This was war.

Passage 7 - What Love Requires

My wife, Bindi, didn't hesitate once I shared this with her.

She volunteered to assist with Tabi's younger sister, Ana. Bindi had much more experience than I did working with kids by this time. That's when she met Dr. Lois Lee, the founder of *Children of the Night*—a national organization well known in the anti-trafficking world. At the time, we had no idea who she was. We'd never connected with official services before. We didn't know how most of the system worked.

But Dr. Lois welcomed us in. She had been Ana's advocate.

This was the first time we touched anything that resembled a system. And although Bindi would one day succeed me as Executive Director of Jonah—after it grew into something far larger—this was where her work truly began.

She became Ana's advocate as well.

That meant sitting with her through the court process. Helping her navigate mental health and medical care. And—most importantly—being someone who wouldn't leave.

It was also the first time we experienced just how broken the system really was.

Ana was offered services—housing, safety, therapy—but only if she agreed to testify in court against her trafficker. That road is almost always treacherous. Victims are often re-traumatized by the legal process, expected to sit in front of their abuser and relive every detail. Convictions are rare. Sentences even rarer. And intimidation alone keeps most girls from ever making it to court.

Ana was no exception.

Dr. Lois requested a police escort so Ana could safely appear and testify. The request was *denied*.

And Ana ran.

The trial was postponed.

It was devastating—but not surprising. We learned early that justice is not automatic. It has to be fought for. And it is almost never clean.

Eventually, the trial did happen. And the pimp went to jail.

Tabi and Ana are living better lives now. Not perfect ones. Not easy ones. But better. They have choices. They have space to breathe. And they are no longer defined by what was done to them.

The work we've done in Spokane since then has helped change some of the policies that failed them—and we'll talk about that later—but this is where the fight began.

The bad news is this: the pimp was a hurting young man himself. We learned he had been taught the trade by his own mother. His brother—the one I had a few tense run-ins with early on—is now dead. Killed in gang violence.

Hurting people hurt people. That has always been true.

But so is this:

Bindi stayed.
Dr. Lois stayed.
And love won.

I can remember one day, a few years later, when Tabi came running into our church, almost shouting, "I need to see Aaron!"

As I stepped away from the pulpit and closed my Bible, my first thought was, *Oh no—what happened?* That was followed immediately by, *Thank God she knew to come find me.* But by the time I reached her, I could tell she was just fine.

She had just been promoted to manager and was opening the store for the first time—but she'd lost her keys. In a panic, she came all the way to church looking for me.

My wife and I, along with a few of the kids from church and a couple of the ladies, gathered around her to reassure her that it was going to be okay. Things like this happen all the time. She would be fine. Her boss would understand. And—oh wow—you're a manager now! Congratulations! This is great.

Tabi walked out of church that morning determined to face this new challenge head-on.

And she did.
And she still does.

Passage 8 — When No One Names It

There are moments when a problem isn't hidden because it's rare. It's hidden because no one has learned how to name it.

That was the reality in Spokane when the Jonah Project began its deeper mission.

Child trafficking wasn't being discussed in schools. It wasn't being addressed from church pulpits or accounted for in city planning. There was no coordinated response, no shared language, no aftercare system waiting for the people who would eventually need it. Not because people were cruel or indifferent, but because the issue itself felt too dark, too complex, or too overwhelming to approach directly.

And that absence mattered.

When adults don't name danger, kids learn to navigate it alone. When institutions avoid uncomfortable conversations, predators fill the gaps. When no one builds a response, survivors are left to improvise their own escape. The absence of a plan isn't neutral—it creates an environment. And environments shape outcomes.

At first, the signs were easy to miss. A student without shoes. A kid sleeping in a car. Teenagers calling late at night, sometimes not even asking for help—just testing whether someone would answer. Then the calls began to change. School counselors reached out quietly, not because they had a protocol, but because they had nothing. A young girl came forward with a story that didn't fit the categories people were used to. Exploitation wasn't happening somewhere else. It was happening here—between kids, through phones, through relationships adults didn't know how to see.

By this time we'd learned to recognize signs; from lifestyles to tattoos. But for most people they still couldn't wrap their minds around the existence of this kind of evil.

Trafficking didn't announce itself as trafficking.
It looked like survival.
It hid behind language like *runaway, prostitution, bad choices.*

And because there was no shared understanding, there was no shared response.

The Jonah Project was a response to that absence.

There was no city task force doing anything except holding small awareness meetings that were not even open to the public. No school district initiative to join. No shelter preparing to receive a trafficked minor at two in the morning. No aftercare programs equipped for trauma layered with fear, loyalty to traffickers, addiction, and grief. There was just a massive wound and immense need..

So the work took whatever shape the need demanded. Answering a phone when shelters were closed. Driving women and children to appointments when they didn't have safer options. Staying present when systems required paperwork survivors didn't have. Learning in real time.

Rescue only existed because no one else was doing it. Aftercare followed because rescue without a place to land causes more harm. Advocacy emerged because survivors were being mislabeled, misunderstood, and mishandled by systems never designed for them. None of this was planned. It was necessary.

Years later, Spokane would declare January Human Trafficking Awareness Month. Billboards would appear. Media coverage would begin to change. Schools would form student groups. Federal agencies would partner in operations. But this awareness didn't create the work. The work had created awareness.

Before a city can name a problem, someone has to step into it quietly—often without recognition, sometimes without funding, and usually without certainty—and stay long enough to understand what's actually happening.

That kind of labor doesn't show up in proclamations or headlines. It happens in living rooms, parking lots, school offices, and downtown bus stations. The work is heavy. The stakes are real. And outcomes are not always within human control.

There was one young girl—we'll call her *Dee*—whose life would eventually reflect every layer of this issue: vulnerability, exploitation, rescue, hope, relapse, and loss. Her story doesn't belong at the beginning of this book, because it isn't an introduction. It's a reckoning. But her life, and her death, remain a reminder that inaction is never neutral—and that refusing to respond carries consequences of its own.

I can remember being told the issue wasn't real, that people were exaggerating, and even by some that I couldn't engage this work without a church's "covering." Reason after reason why I should look the other way too, or throw my hands up. Or wait for someone else to step up.

The first thing I learned in that season was that if you wait for permission to respond, you will always arrive too late.

It was somewhere around these early developments that I realized we needed a name. I get asked often why we call it The Jonah Project. I think some folks intuitively guess it has to do with Jonah from The Bible – and they're mostly right. Jonah was asked by God to go somewhere new, scary and dangerous, and do something other people like him would balk at. And Jonah ran. It was kind of how I was feeling in the early days when I realized God was asking me to go into the dark places I'd spent my whole life trying to escape. If I had my dithers I'd preach the Gospel in Maui or Bali or Fiji or some other beautiful locale. And there'd be a paycheck and less sacrifice from my wife and kids. It's really a big question when you have a God who prizes free will like He does. So when thinking of what I'd call our little experiment in kindness, truth be told I was frustrated and making fun of myself and the community. Making fun of resources that just couldn't seem to get over themselves enough to do what they were really being called to do. So, tongue in cheek and with a smart-assed nod at our churches, our nonprofits and ourselves – I called it The Jonah Project.

Everything that followed—the rescues, the international work, the partnerships, the failures of systems, and the moments of undeniable grace—supported that truth. What changed Spokane wasn't a plan that finally appeared. It was people who finally refused to look away once they saw what was there.

Passage 9 — The Critical Figure

Exploitation doesn't begin with violence.
It begins with replacement.

Every person needs a critical figure in their life—someone who provides safety, attention, guidance, affirmation, and a sense of belonging. When that figure is absent, inconsistent, overwhelmed, or unsafe, something else will eventually move in to fill the space.

In the lives of many of the kids and women Jonah encountered, that space already existed long before exploitation began. A father gone. A mother working constantly. A home shaped by addiction, instability, or neglect. Not always malicious—often just overwhelmed. But the absence was real.

Absence is not neutral.

It is an invitation

Grooming works because it doesn't feel like harm at first. It feels like attention. Like protection. Like someone finally noticing. The trafficker doesn't arrive announcing control. They arrive offering what appears to be care. Over time, they become the critical figure—the one whose approval matters, whose voice carries weight, whose presence feels necessary for survival.

That is why leaving is so difficult.

From the outside, it's easy to ask why someone doesn't just walk away. But when the person exploiting you has replaced the role of safety, identity, or belonging in your life, walking away feels like losing the only anchor you have—even if that anchor is slowly pulling you under.

This is why rescue alone is never enough.

What Jonah learned—slowly, carefully, and often counter to instinct—was that the first work was not extraction. It was presence. Real, consistent, non-judgmental presence that did not demand anything in return.

Advocates showed up not as saviors, but as steady alternatives.

They answered calls.
They sat through silence.
They held on when stories contradicted themselves.
They didn't flinch when loyalty to the trafficker surfaced.
They didn't rush disclosure or push decisions.

And over time, something subtle began to happen.

A text asking if someone wanted to grab a milkshake.
A question about going to a movie.
A hesitant request to come along to church—not for belief, but for belonging.

To outsiders, these moments can look like opportunities for influence. But the deeper truth is simpler and more human: the critical figure was beginning to shift.

This wasn't manipulation.
It was replacement through trust.

By being present without leverage, advocates slowly eroded the belief that the person causing harm was the only one who could be trusted. The nervous system began to recalibrate. The survival brain began to imagine alternatives. And the natural defenses that exploitation suppresses started to wake back up.

This process takes time.
It requires restraint.
And it demands something from the advocate that can't be faked.

Because when you step into the role of a critical figure—even temporarily—you are walking with someone through confusion, attachment, grief, and fear. You can't rush that. You can't control it. And you can't carry it unless you are grounded in something deeper than yourself.

For Jonah, faith mattered here—not as a tool for conversion, but as an anchor. Advocates had to be rooted enough to stay steady while someone else found their footing. To walk with a survivor until the critical figure in their life could slowly become themselves—or, in time, something even stronger.

Showing up this way is costly.
But not showing up is never neutral.

If an advocate doesn't fill the space, someone else will. And that "someone else" will almost always have an agenda.

Passage 10 — Relocation Was Refuge

Rescue and relocation was never the plan.

Relocation was something I had the skills to do and early on before there was a team or housing resource, the one thing I could do was go and get the child or the lady out of bondage.

It emerged because presence, on its own, eventually reached its limits. Trust could open doors. Advocacy could steady someone's footing. But there were moments when staying nearby was no longer enough—when danger was no longer theoretical, and waiting became its own form of harm.

Those moments didn't announce themselves clearly.

They arrived as escalation. A change in tone during a phone call. A sudden silence where there had once been daily contact. A new name mentioned too casually. A ride offered by someone no one had met. Control tightening beneath the surface of what still looked, from the outside, like choice.

This was the space where Jonah found itself standing—not eager, not prepared, but unwilling to pretend that proximity alone could keep someone safe.

In the beginning, Jonah was not a team.

There were no partnerships yet. No shared protocols. No established roles. The work moved forward simply because someone had to step into that space, and at that time, I was the one available.

Long before pastoring or coaching baseball, my life had taken me through seasons that involved training in hostage rescue, executive protection, and high-risk security environments. Those experiences weren't sought out with this work in mind, but they shaped how I approached threat assessment, planning, restraint, and responsibility when the need arose. I learned from professionals in the field—people like Nirmalya Bhowmick—whose influence emphasized preparation, discretion, and control over force.

That background didn't make the work easy.
It made it possible to approach it carefully.

Rescue is not about confrontation.
It is about regulation.

Lowering your heartbeat.
Reading a room before entering it.
Knowing exits, basements, alleyways, and fences.
Moving gently enough not to increase the fear of a child who is already terrified.

The real danger was never bravado.
It was panic, miscalculation, and ego.

Early on, people would offer to help. Men with impressive credentials. Military experience. Weapons. One pastor asked if he could come along carrying a high-powered rifle, not realizing that doing so would draw fire toward the very people we were trying to protect.

That kind of help had to be refused.

Because the measure of readiness was never strength. It was gentleness under pressure. The ability to hold the hand of an eleven-year-old without escalating her fear. The discipline to de-escalate rather than dominate.

Rescues had to be planned and briefed carefully. We were not law enforcement. We had to be invited in. Often, the only intelligence available came from the victim herself—partial details whispered from inside a dangerous place. A street name. The color of the house next door. A chain-link fence. A basement entrance. Enough to act, but never enough to be certain.

And still, the work had to be done.

Law-enforcement calls placed by victims were often routed as domestic disturbances. Temporary interventions. No lasting care. No advocate waiting on the other side. The gap between danger and safety was wide, and someone had to step into it.

That gap eventually carried us beyond Spokane.

One rescue stands out for a number of reasons. It was the furthest I ever went to bring a woman home—and it was also two other things at once: one of the clearest examples of institutional failure I've ever witnessed, and one of our greatest success stories.

The largest ministry in Spokane contacted me about two women sleeping in their shelter. Through intake and conversation, they discovered both women had been trafficked. One had been trafficked through Texas for ten years. When she finally got out, she headed for what she believed was a hotel job in Florida. The job waiting for her wasn't housekeeping. She was trafficked again—this time for another seven years—until an FBI bust freed her.

With no money and no resources, she bought a bus ticket as far west from Miami as she could go. That's how she ended up in Spokane. She spoke no English. Since I spoke some Spanish, I was able to help..

At first, I wasn't sure what role Jonah could play. We weren't trying to replace the shelter—just augment what wasn't there. One of the women was quickly connected to a Spanish-speaking church. She blossomed. Within a few months—and a few new outfits—she didn't need much from us. She had found community. Family. Watching that happen was a gift.

The other woman—Maria—had been trafficked between Washington and international borders- and was still carrying layers of trauma that surfaced the moment she spoke. Somewhere, she had a mother who held custody of her children. Maria dreamed of being healthy enough to be their mom again. She wanted them to be proud of her—not ashamed.

During our first conversation, I had to gently interrupt her. It was clear that retelling her story was pulling her back into the trauma. What she shared was graphic and violent—things done to her, things she had witnessed.

This work was slow. Careful.

Bindi came alongside as her advocate, and something began to shift. Maria bonded deeply with my wife. She got sober. Her eyes were bright again. And when you've watched people struggle for years with addiction or insomnia, seeing someone respond that quickly to safety and trust—it's nothing short of a miracle.

Eventually, Maria was accepted into a long-term housing program affiliated with a large local charity. It was structured. It was safe.

And it came with a catch.

They instituted a blackout period—thirty to ninety days with no outside contact. The policy was designed to sever ties with dealers, abusers, enablers. But in Maria's case, the only safe attachments she had were suddenly removed: Bindi, and a few women from our church.

She begged for an exception. Sunday church. One hour with Bindi. They said no.

Bindi advocated for her—walking with Maria to mental-health appointments, helping her through daily recovery steps—but before anything could be resolved, Maria became overwhelmed.

She left the facility.

We didn't know. We believed she was still there, enduring the blackout period.

Then one day, I got a call.

A shaky voice. A borrowed phone. Maria.

She was in the bed of a truck, hiding under blankets, in another country..

I won't share locations or details. But I will say this: it became one of the most defining journeys I've ever taken. The threat level was real. I was crossing a border alone, with little time to plan. Although Maria was a U.S. citizen, her documents had been taken by the men who controlled her.

I let a DHS contact know I was going. He wished me well and gave me his cell number. I didn't realize then how much I'd need it.

This was our first international operation. Jonah's mission had always been local. Eventually, it would grow into something broader. But Maria was one of ours—and she had called.

This was where our words became action.

I still remember passing my sons on the stairs before I left. Tommy Boy had tears in his eyes. Calvin was quiet, somber. And Kahlil—my youngest—looked at me and said, "Dad, I trust you. Just don't write a check your body can't cash."

Wise beyond his years.

I told them, "God's going to walk us through the gates of hell and back with a story."

And He did.

That journey wasn't accomplished alone. Two Jonah members—one of our advocates and a close friend—helped coordinate buses, hotels, and logistics from afar. Tim handled critical communication and planning. It was collaboration at its best.

Today, Maria's smile is bright. Her future is brighter still. At the time of this writing, I've learned she's expecting her first grandchild.

And now when she crosses borders, it's on vacation—with her kids.

Passage 11 — The Best Ability is Availability

I had decided to get a second line.

Girls I'd helped would pass my number along—quietly, cautiously. Sometimes it was a school counselor. Sometimes it was a friend of a friend. But every time, the voice on the other end was scared, tired, and looking for a way out.

So I bought a second phone—just for them.

Looking back, I probably should've prayed about it first.

I didn't think about burnout or boundaries or logistics. I just knew there were kids out there—in parking lots, bathrooms, side streets—trying to make a call before the wrong person noticed.

Sometimes it was a friend's phone.
Sometimes it was a borrowed charger at Domino's.

Wherever they were, they knew what they'd heard from me or a friend:

If you call, I will come. No matter how bad the situation is. No matter how dangerous the person hurting you is. No matter where you are. No matter what.

The calls were anything.

Sometimes it was a student who had nowhere to go that night—sleeping in a car, couch surfing, or walking the streets. We'd learned quickly that homelessness makes kids immediate targets. More than twenty percent of homeless teens will report being trafficked—and often within forty-eight hours of becoming homeless. That clock starts fast. Too fast.

Other times it was an assistant principal calling quietly to say a student had just returned to school after missing for a week. A girl who sat down in an office and told a harrowing story—being held against her will, unable to leave, and this time a baby was involved.

Those calls could overwhelm you—if you had time to be overwhelmed.

But you don't.

The line doesn't ring when you're ready. It rings when someone is desperate. And there's no pause button for fear.

At first it was two or three calls a week.

Then the line started ringing during dinner. During holidays. Even in the middle of my son's high school graduation.

I got a call right as they were lining up the seniors to receive their diplomas.

By then, I'd started getting some help.

I had begun training a few men I trusted—men who shared the heart of the work, who weren't afraid of chaos, and who understood this wasn't about being a hero. It was about being available. They weren't saviors any more than I was—a mental health nurse, a real-estate appraiser, a pastor's brother—but they were men whose integrity I knew I could trust.

That day, two of them handled the relocation.

And I got to watch my son walk the stage.

The Resource Line never had office hours.
It didn't come with grant funding or a call center.

It was just a phone.
Held in the hand of someone who said yes.

And here's the truth I learned along the way:

I don't save anybody.
That's God's job.

We learned early—from experience and from conversations I'd had with our local FBI liaison—that getting someone out doesn't mean they stay out. A person can walk away three or four times before they truly walk free.

So my job was to make sure they had free choices.

To stand in the gap long enough for that person to breathe again.
To see themselves clearly.
To remember their worth.

That's the heart of real advocacy.

Not controlling their decisions—
but defending their right to make them.

And yes, many of the young women we served eventually chose to walk with Jesus. That never surprised me.

But what God asked of me wasn't to convert anyone.

It was to make sure that no man ever put his hands on them again without their consent.

That's what we fought for.
That's what the second line was for.

Not to save.

But to stand in the gap—long enough for freedom to become a real choice.

And on the other side of those calls—after the chaos, after the long nights—there were moments that reminded us why we kept answering.

Watching a father's knees buckle in gratitude when reunited with his daughter.
Seeing a mother's soul lift as the light returned to her child's eyes.
Families reconnected.
Breathing again.

Moments that reminded us that God is bigger than all of this—even when we felt small compared to the tide of need and brokenness.

Especially then.

Passage 12 — Aftercare Was the Point

Aftercare didn't emerge as a surprise.
It was the reason the work existed in the first place.

From the beginning, advocacy meant walking alongside someone. Not awareness campaigns or public conversations—those mattered, but they were never the core of the work. Advocacy meant walking with someone after the moment of crisis had passed, when the adrenaline faded and the real work began.

That truth was clear after the very first girl Jonah helped.

Before anything scaled, before partnerships or rescues beyond Spokane, there was study. Listening. Reading survivor testimony. Talking with other organizations who had been in this space longer. Everywhere the same reality surfaced: people wanted to help, but no one had a place for survivors to go.

There were programs.
There were task forces.
There were grants.

But there was no housing.

Care was fragmented. Survivors were moved from system to system, expected to heal while navigating bureaucracy, instability, and pressure to "progress." Resources existed, but they weren't connected. And without someone walking alongside them, survivors were often left to carry the weight alone.

What Jonah set out to build was not a single solution, but a **holistic one**.

Advocacy meant connection—to counseling, education, medical care, job placement, spiritual community, and, when it was healthy, reconnection with family who wanted them home. Rescue moved people out of immediate danger, but advocacy was what moved them toward a life that could actually hold.

    Rescue was the vehicle.
Aftercare was the destination.

    Housing quickly became the most urgent expression of that truth. Without a safe place to land, nothing else could take root. You can't attend counseling if you don't know where you'll sleep. You can't finish school if you're constantly being relocated. You can't begin to trust if every door closes after a few days.

    So staying became the work.

    What made this possible—what puzzled other organizations even more than the scope of the work—was that it was done almost entirely by volunteers.

    Every advocate, including myself, served without pay.

    Other groups, some with funding and small paid teams, struggled to sustain the work. More than once, we were asked how it was possible that Jonah operated with dozens of volunteers when others could not—even with resources.

    The answer was simpler than it sounded.

    Everyone had a place at the table.

    Volunteers weren't treated as temporary labor or kept at arm's length. They were trusted, trained, and invited into the work meaningfully. Teachers, real estate agents, parents, students—people from every walk of life—were given responsibility and dignity, not just tasks.

Advocacy didn't belong to a professional class.
It belonged to a community.

Because the work was relational, people stayed. Because the mission was clear, people gave generously of their time. And because survivors were treated as human beings rather than projects, advocates didn't burn out trying to manage outcomes they were never meant to control.

But aftercare carried a cost that wasn't immediately visible.

It was here—not in rescue, but in staying—that I first encountered what would later be called compassion fatigue and vicarious trauma. Building the first safe home took more out of me than I expected. In the span of a month, I lost nearly thirty pounds under the weight of the responsibility. Not from fear, but from the constant pressure of holding space for pain that didn't turn off at night.

I wasn't alone in that.

Our advocates—many of them ordinary people with generous hearts—were stepping into depths they had never been trained to navigate. They were absorbing stories of abuse, loss, betrayal, and grief, often without realizing how deeply it was affecting them. Loving well came with a toll on the human heart.

It became clear that aftercare could not stop with survivors.
If the work was going to last, we had to care for the caregivers too.

So I began to say the same things to the team, again and again.

Rest when you can.
Be honest about your own needs.
Let the team rally around you and pray for you.
Seek God deeply in prayer, because no one can carry this alone.

And above all, demand only one thing of yourself: love the person in front of you the best you can with the time you have—and leave the rest to God.

That posture changed everything.

Advocates didn't have to save anyone. They didn't have to fix outcomes or carry guilt for things beyond their control. Faithfulness, not effectiveness, became the measure. Presence, not perfection.

This kind of care was slow.
It was demanding.
And it could not be rushed.

Aftercare wasn't about fixing people. It was about creating conditions where healing could happen without pressure or performance. Where survivors weren't treated as problems to be solved, but as people worth the long road back.

That approach didn't make the work easier.
It made it honest.

Aftercare wasn't a phase that followed rescue.
It was the work that gave rescue meaning.

And it only worked because no one—survivor or advocate—was left on the outside of it.

Passage 13 — A Place at The Table

Trauma trains people to survive systems, not trust them.

By the time many survivors reached Jonah, they had learned how to comply, perform, and disappear inside expectations that were never designed for their healing. Control had been disguised as care so many times that safety itself felt suspicious. Rules had always come with consequences. Help has always come with a price.

So Jonah learned early that control could not be the tool of healing.

Belonging had to come first.

This was not intuitive. Most systems are built around compliance: follow the program, meet the benchmarks, demonstrate progress. But trauma doesn't respond to efficiency. It responds to consistency. And consistency only works when people are not afraid of being discarded the moment they falter.

Belonging changes the nervous system before it changes behavior.

In homes, schools, and everyday spaces, survivors were offered something many had never experienced: a place where they were allowed to exist without proving anything. No performance. No pressure to disclose. No expectation of gratitude. Just a seat at the table that didn't disappear when things got messy.

This kind of belonging didn't appear by accident.

God provided it through people.

A small church willing to be stretched beyond comfort. People who were willing to learn, to be trained, and to take responsibility for loving well. By this point, the work was no longer informal. Clear practices were already in place—everything from what a survivor needed in the first seventy-two hours of care, to medical attention, dietary considerations, medication management, and the use of interpreters when necessary. A written manual existed because clarity mattered—not just for survivors, but for those caring for them.

Liberty, our first house mom, stepped into that structure with steadiness and courage, carrying both compassion and discipline when the work demanded both. The Holmes family opened their home to *Dee*—and gave her a place where safety wasn't conditional and belonging wasn't fragile. They didn't fix her story. They lived it with her.

And alongside my wife, Bindi, God raised up advocates who would carry the work far beyond what I could have imagined. Michelina, in particular, became a constant presence—grounded, fierce, and compassionate—eventually serving as lead advocate and working shoulder to shoulder with Bindi as the work grew in both depth and scale.

None of this was accidental.
All of it was necessary.

This wasn't permissiveness.
It was safety without coercion.

There were moments when this philosophy was tested.

A teenage girl staying in one of our safe homes went out one night with friends and didn't come back. She smoked marijuana. She broke curfew. She violated the rules everyone knew. In most programs, that would have been the end. Disqualification. Removal. Consequences delivered from a distance. Even well-meaning organizations often respond by reallocating resources or severing ties in moments like these.

Jonah made a different call.

We called her home.

Yes, she made a mistake.
Yes, she broke the rules.
And yes, all of that still mattered.

But none of it mattered more than making sure she didn't disappear back into the hands of people who were waiting to take her. The bad guys are always watching for moments like that—when shame isolates and systems reject. We chose to say something else instead: *Come home. You are loved. We will work through this together, safely, with people who are for you.*

That decision forced a question we had to answer again and again.

What is more valuable—our program, or our people?

When people are no longer bracing for removal, something shifts. Defensiveness softens. Hypervigilance eases. The constant calculation of what is required to stay begins to fade. That space—quiet and often invisible—is where real healing begins.

Control can create compliance.
It cannot create trust.

Belonging, on the other hand, invites participation. Survivors began to make choices not because they were forced to, but because they felt secure enough to risk agency. Small decisions mattered. When to talk. When to rest. Who to trust. Whether to engage with counseling, school, work, or faith.

Freedom had to be modeled before it could be embraced.

This approach frustrated some observers. Progress didn't look linear. Healing didn't follow timelines. Setbacks weren't treated as failures. But Jonah had learned that rushing recovery often recreates the very power dynamics survivors were trying to escape.

Belonging requires patience.

It also requires restraint from those offering care. The temptation to manage outcomes—to push, fix, or rescue again—had to be resisted. Advocates learned to walk at someone else's pace, even when that pace felt painfully slow.

What surprised many was how much this posture healed advocates as well.

When people were no longer expected to control outcomes, they were free to love without fear of failure. Presence replaced pressure. Faithfulness replaced effectiveness. Community formed not around success stories, but around shared humanity.

Belonging worked in both directions.

Survivors weren't the only ones who needed a place to stand. Advocates did too. And when everyone was allowed to be fully human—limited, learning, and dependent on grace—the work became sustainable.

This is why leverage-free care mattered so deeply.

Control would have been faster.
Programs would have been easier to measure.

But belonging was the only thing strong enough to undo what exploitation had taught.

Healing didn't happen because survivors were managed well.
It happened because they were not managed at all.

They were welcomed.
They were stayed with.
They were trusted to become who they were created to be.

Belonging healed what control never could.

Passage 14 — Diamond in the Snow

Early on, we hadn't relocated anyone to another living situation outside of Spokane.
But we would learn—quickly—that relocation would become one of our most important tools.

Getting a survivor to safety isn't just about shelter.
It's about distance.

Distance from the pain.
Distance from the people who caused it.
And distance from the systems that often fail to keep them safe.

I'd seen it happen before.

A girl is finally on her way to healing—on the bus to school, or standing in a social services office applying for food stamps—and she runs into her pimp. Or a dealer. Or one of the men who hurt her. Maybe they just say something. Maybe they grab her arm.

Either way, she's gone—either retraumatized or pulled straight back into captivity.

I got a call from a girl I'd helped before.

I hadn't seen her in some time. She told me she was doing okay, living with family out of state. She said she had a friend she thought needed help.

After she explained the situation, I told her of course I would help. Then I sat down to pray.

After praying, I decided to call my close friend Alana Holmes.

I told her I was going to pick up a seventeen-year-old girl in a bad spot. It was November, and it was freezing outside. At the time, all I knew was that she needed a place to stay that night. I didn't know the whole story. I wasn't aware of any immediate threats—if I had been, I wouldn't have asked Alana to help.

Alana listened. Then she said, "We're in."

Even better, her husband Nick offered to drive and said we could take their truck.

Nick had been a tank commander in the Army. He's one of my favorite people on the planet. He and Alana are salt-of-the-earth folk—courageous, loyal, no-nonsense. They don't play church. They live it. They're family to me, to Bindi, to my boys.

That night, they became family to someone else too.

We showed up at a small house not even a mile from the high school.

There was snow on the ground, and three black garbage bags lined the walkway.

A young girl opened the door—African American, bright eyes, beautiful smile.
She introduced herself as Dee.

Over her shoulder, I saw four young men—lounging, gaming, barely noticing.
An older woman appeared from the back hallway. She said nothing.

Indifferent. Detached.

Later, I would learn who she was—one of several "caretakers" in town who let kids stay in exchange for EBT cards, access to social services, and far too often, sexual favors.

Dee had been living there.

With her things packed in garbage bags.
With four grown boys and one indifferent adult.
Just god-awful circumstances.

I introduced myself. Dee seemed a little surprised.
She laughed and said, "I thought you were Black—you sound Black on the phone."

And she laughed again.

Dee had a hearty laugh. A belly laugh.
She was tiny, but her laugh could fill a room.

Assessing the scene, I looked at Nick and Alana. We didn't need to say anything.
We all knew: she's not staying here another minute.

We told Dee she'd stay with Nick and Alana that night, and that we'd figure everything else out tomorrow.

Then, as we walked back to the truck, she stopped and bent over.

Those three black garbage bags in the snow?
Those were her belongings.

Nick and I looked at each other—and for a brief moment, we both thought the same thing:
someone needs to get dragged out into this snow and taught a lesson.

But we kept our cool.

We let Alana lead.
And we got Dee out of there.

Later that night, Alana called.

She and Nick had talked it over and decided: Dee was staying.

The Holmes family loved her like a daughter. I loved her very much too, and I still do.

I can still remember the night we met her like it was yesterday. I remember the Waffle House where I'd take her for hangouts and catch-ups. I remember the day in that Waffle House parking lot when she cried out to God for the first time—the anguish of her hurt and the promise of healing it held.

There's more about this kiddo in the story.

Because out of the hundreds and hundreds of survivors The Jonah Project has served, no one has taught us more about what human trafficking looks like. And no child we have served has experienced more complete and systemic failure—on the part of the city, law enforcement, the courts, and her biological family—than Dee did.

But that night?

That night she got out.

And she laughed.

Passage 15 — Learning to Be Free

Freedom doesn't move at the speed we wish it would.

Once the immediate danger has passed, once a survivor is safe and the crisis quiets, a new temptation appears—the urge to hurry healing along. To measure progress. To look for signs that the work is paying off. To believe that enough care, applied correctly, will produce predictable results.

Trauma does not cooperate with that impulse.

For people whose lives have been shaped by exploitation, freedom unfolds slowly, often unevenly. Forward movement is rarely straight. Growth is interrupted by fear, memory, attachment, and grief. Old coping mechanisms resurface not because healing has failed, but because the nervous system is still learning what safety actually means.

This is where many systems lose patience.

Setbacks are labeled resistance.
Relapse is treated as regression.
Return is interpreted as ingratitude.

But Jonah learned something different by staying long enough to see the pattern repeat.

When survivors stepped back toward what was familiar—even when that familiarity had once harmed them—it wasn't because they preferred pain. It was because familiarity feels predictable, and predictability feels safe to a traumatized brain. Freedom, by contrast, can feel terrifying. It requires choice, responsibility, and the risk of disappointment.

That's why rushing freedom often drives people back into bondage.

Jonah learned to expect this—not as failure, but as part of the process. Some survivors left and came back. Some disappeared for months and returned quietly. Some tested boundaries repeatedly, not to defy care, but to see whether it would survive their worst moments.

Patience became the discipline.

Advocates had to learn how to stay present without chasing outcomes. To welcome someone back without shaming them for leaving. To hold boundaries without weaponizing them. To speak truth without withdrawing love.

This kind of patience costs more than urgency ever does.

It asks caregivers to surrender control over timelines. It demands humility in the face of unfinished stories. It requires faith that God is working even when progress isn't visible.

For girls like *Dee*—this lesson unfolded over time.

Freedom didn't arrive all at once. It came in fragments. Moments of clarity followed by seasons of confusion. Hope interrupted by grief. Courage undermined by attachment. Each step forward exposed new layers of pain that had been buried beneath survival.

Staying with her meant resisting the urge to define her story too soon.

It meant allowing her to be unfinished.

That was hard. For everyone.

Because unfinished stories don't reassure us. They don't provide clean endings or inspirational conclusions. They force us to live with uncertainty and to trust God with outcomes we cannot control.

But this is where the deepest work happened.

When survivors realized they were not being measured by progress charts or compliance milestones, something shifted. The pressure to perform eased. The fear of being cut loose diminished. Space opened for honesty—for naming doubt, anger, longing, and confusion without fear of consequences.

Freedom grew there.

Not quickly.
Not cleanly.
But genuinely.

Jonah learned that the goal was never to produce independent success stories on a schedule. The goal was to create enough safety for people to choose freedom for themselves, again and again, even when it was hard.

Freedom cannot be rushed.
It must be trusted.

And trusting freedom requires faith—faith that God is patient, that His work is not hurried, and that love applied steadily over time is stronger than any single moment of rescue.

This lesson reshaped everything.

It slowed the work.
It deepened relationships.
And it taught Jonah that staying—through relapse, return, and unfinished endings—was not a weakness.

It was the work.

Passage 16 — Crossing the Bridge

Someone emailed me a link one day and suggested I think about applying for the Spokane Human Rights Commission.

At first, I wasn't sure. That didn't feel like my world. I was a coach. A mentor. A guy who answered the phone when someone was in trouble.

But I kept thinking about it.

Could we get human trafficking taken seriously?
Could local law enforcement finally listen?
Could we—without forcing victims to relive their pain publicly—convince the city to admit they didn't have a plan, but that they would try to make one?

Any kind of recognition would be a win.

So I filled out the online application.

I brought with me a letter of recommendation from Dee—nineteen years old now—and went downtown to City Hall to meet Mayor David Condon, who would ultimately decide whether I'd receive the appointment.

The conversation was easy. I found him to be a decent man. He said he was becoming more aware of trafficking as an issue in our city and that he'd like to see Spokane do something meaningful about it.

When the interview ended, I stood to leave.

As I turned toward the door, he stopped me.

"Do you have any questions for me?"

I looked at him, then at the folder on his desk, and said,

"Mayor, in that folder is my résumé and a recommendation letter from a nineteen-year-old girl named Dee. My only question is this: what would you say to her if she were standing here instead of me? If she asked you how to navigate this scary, complicated world—what would you tell her to do when she feels overwhelmed, alone, or lost?"

He paused.

Then he said, "I suppose I'd tell her to find a community. A church, or a family group maybe—somewhere she could trust."

He smiled.

I nodded and headed out.

Not thinking about shaping the future of the city—but knowing in my heart that God sees these victims. And that somehow, He had a plan for them to be heard.

I crossed the Monroe Street Bridge heading north, driving home, thinking about miracles.

Passage 17 — Lighthouse

About this time, something incredible happened.

I had a breakfast meeting with a woman named Kristi Burns, who served on the board at Life Center Church—one of Spokane's largest congregations. She listened as I shared what we were doing, asked honest questions, and then said something I'll never forget:

"We believe in this. We're in."

Life Center became our first official sponsor, donating $1,000 a month to support the work. It wasn't just the money—though that mattered. It was the affirmation. Someone saw what we were doing and believed in it. They didn't ask for metrics or demand reports. They simply said, "Keep going."

With that gift, and a few other monthly donors stepping up with twenty dollars here, a hundred dollars there, we were finally able to open our own safe home.

We called it **Lighthouse**.

Lighthouse was the most galvanizing community engagement we had seen in Spokane around this issue to date. Multiple high schools began calling us. Counselors shared resources—and suddenly, we were the resource. It wasn't orchestrated. It was organic. Our team grew stronger, and the volunteer base expanded quickly.

We had to be careful as we put the house together. It needed to stay safe. It needed to stay quiet. But I remember one of our relocation guys painting all day alongside one of his kids, who had asked if they could help. I remember the joy on people's faces as they worked to build what would become Spokane's first truly operational safe home for victims of trafficking.

Lighthouse would go on to serve scores of local girls, as well as young women we relocated from other parts of the country where they weren't safe.

It became a beacon.

Other ministries began reaching out, and now we were in a position to help someone else by offering a real resource. For the first time, the city had a place to point to when a girl needed somewhere safe to land.

The crazy thing is—Lighthouse almost didn't happen.

When that first $1,000 donation came in, nearly every pastor I knew told me the same thing: *God is blessing your family. This should be your first salary.* They meant well. The time we'd invested and the risks we'd taken felt, to them, like they were finally being repaid.

But what the kids needed was more than a shelter or a temporary solution. They needed to know what *home* felt like.

I remember talking it over with Liberty and with my wife, Bindi. We all came to the same conclusion: God would provide for us. But this money was enough to get a three-bedroom house.

So that's what we did.

Liberty Allen—one of our first advocates—became Jonah's first house mom. She didn't just manage the house. She loved those kids like they were her own. She knew how to hold boundaries without ever withholding grace. Her presence gave Lighthouse warmth, structure, and safety.

We had a home.
We had a team.
We had momentum.

The calls came in all forms.

Sometimes it was a school counselor asking for help with transportation or mental health referrals. Other times it was more urgent—a teenage girl stuck at a bus station at three in the morning, or someone trying to escape an abusive partner before he got home from work.

I remember one call from a young woman whose trafficker had just been arrested. She was terrified he'd make bail and come find her. We picked her up within the hour and relocated her out of town. Another time, I helped a girl move her belongings out of an apartment after her roommate—a man she barely knew—became increasingly threatening. She was eighteen. She didn't have anyone else.

Every story was different.
But the approach never changed.

No leverage.
No pressure.
Just: *You're not alone.*

And Bindi was right there with me whenever she could be. At that point, we didn't have money to pay her. But she never needed a paycheck to care. Her heart was always in it, and the girls knew it.

These were the early days.

Scrappy.
Raw.
Real.

And God was in every single step.

Passage 18 — City Hall

I had been serving on the Spokane Human Rights Commission for a while by then.

I'd done some educating. Some informing. But truthfully, we hadn't gained much traction. People would nod. They'd listen politely. But nothing was really moving.

Then one day, Dee came to me and said she wanted to speak to the commission. She wanted to tell them what it was we were fighting for.

I was hesitant. I needed to be sure she wasn't feeling pressured to share her story. But she was determined.

That was one thing about Dee—she carried her pain with purpose. She was grateful for her second chance, and she loved Jonah like it was her family. She used to tell me all the time, "We have to keep going, Aaron. So other girls don't end up like I did."

So we went.

And she spoke.

There wasn't a dry eye in the room. The commission sat in stunned silence as she told them about being tied up in a basement for a week. About being forced full of drugs and alcohol until she threw up. About knowing—without a doubt—that there were more girls like her in Spokane right now, waiting for someone to show up.

It was one of the heaviest nights we ever experienced.

And it changed almost nothing.

The room was moved. That much was clear. But when the meeting ended, we were right back to parking ordinances and housing code updates.

It was as if the issue was too heavy for anyone to know what to do with it. And so, once again, it was set aside.

Eventually, we were given time with City Councilmember Lori Kinnear.

And she listened. Really listened.

She asked if we would help draft a city resolution addressing human trafficking. Truthfully, Lori needed something tangible—something she could point to, something that gave her political traction. The resolution did that. She would go on to reference it in future campaigns.

But the promise to go deeper—to pass something with real weight, like a city ordinance—never materialized.

Mayor David Condon left office without ever meaningfully addressing human trafficking again.

Then came Mayor Nadine Woodward. She sat in my church office for an hour, promising to make the issue a priority. She said all the right things. And then disappeared until the next campaign cycle.

Still, one day there we were—forty or so Jonah advocates, all wearing our new Jonah t-shirts—filling the seats at City Hall. Spokane's first-ever resolution supporting trafficking survivors was on the agenda.

It wasn't perfect. It didn't have teeth.

But it was something.

A beginning. A public acknowledgment. Awareness raised in a way that couldn't be undone.

That day, I'll never forget the moment my son Calvin leaned over and whispered, "Dad… can I go speak?"

I nodded.

And I sat there—just a dad in a room full of people—watching my seventeen-year-old son walk up to the podium and speak truth to power.

He talked about language. About how we needed to stop calling children *prostitutes*. About how kids caught in trafficking weren't criminals. They were victims. Survivors. People worth fighting for.

I've worked alongside many courageous people.

But that day, my son stood among the bravest.

Passage 19 — Kids Saving Kids

One of the most unexpected gifts Jonah received didn't come from donors or institutions.

It came from schools.

High school counselors were among our earliest and strongest allies. Not because they were trained for this kind of work—but because they were already carrying far more than their job descriptions allowed. They were the ones seeing kids disappear for weeks and come back different. The ones piecing together stories that didn't make sense on paper. The ones who knew something was wrong long before anyone else wanted to say it out loud.

They didn't have many options.

So when Jonah showed up—without paperwork, without pitch decks, without conditions—they leaned in.

Counselors became connectors. Quiet advocates. Bridge-builders between kids and safety. They called when they weren't supposed to have a solution yet. They trusted us with stories that couldn't be unspoken once heard. And they stayed—long after the crisis had passed—checking in, following up, making sure kids didn't fall back through the cracks.

And then something even more surprising happened.

Students noticed.

High school bands organized donation drives—collecting clothes, hygiene items, and basic necessities. Not because they were assigned to. Because they cared. Student groups formed Jonah Clubs—young people choosing to educate themselves and each other, choosing to talk openly about exploitation, choosing to see what was easier to ignore.

That took courage.

These weren't safe topics. They weren't popular causes. Talking about trafficking meant talking about uncomfortable truths—about classmates, about systems, about adults failing to protect kids. And still, they stepped forward.

What mattered wasn't the size of the donations or the scale of the events.

It was the posture.

They refused to look away.

None of this happened because Jonah had the most resources or the best funding. We didn't. It happened because God was building something that wasn't transactional—it was relational.

There were no sign-up requirements.
No thresholds to meet.
No proof of worthiness demanded.

There was simply room.

Room for counselors to care without being alone.
Room for students to act without being patronized.
Room for schools to participate without being blamed.

God wasn't asking anyone for credentials.

He was asking for hearts.

And the truth is—anyone can build a relationship.

That's what made Jonah accessible. It didn't belong to professionals or experts. It belonged to people willing to show up, stay present, and refuse to pretend they hadn't seen what they'd seen.

These counselors, students, and schools weren't accessories to the work.

They were the work.

And in choosing not to look away, they became part of a story far bigger than any one organization—a story where love multiplied simply because people said yes.

Passage 20 — Freedom Railroad

As Jonah grew, so did the need for something more consistent.

The rescue line was still active, but the calls were coming from farther away now—across the region, sometimes from out of state. We had built trust with other ministries, youth advocates, school counselors, and safe-home coordinators across the Pacific Northwest.

But the same problem kept showing up.

Resources were limited.
And housing almost always came with strings attached.

We needed something better.
Something built for this.

That's where the idea for the **Freedom Railroad** was born.

Not a single place—but a pathway.

The model was simple, but it required humility. No one organization could do everything well. No single house, church, or program could carry the full weight of rescue, aftercare, advocacy, and restoration on its own.

So instead of building one more centralized solution, we began building connections.

We called them **HUBs**.

Each HUB offered a piece of the care puzzle. One location might provide housing. Another might be a church trained in trauma-informed advocacy. Another might offer financial support, transportation, or long-term mentorship. Individually, none of them were enough.

Together, they were powerful.

We began building HUBs across Washington—north, west, wherever people were ready. I visited churches and organizations that wanted to help but didn't know how to step in safely. Most were willing. They just needed guidance. They needed permission to engage without fear of getting it wrong.

By then, we had walked through enough—trial, heartbreak, failure, prayer—that we had something honest to share. Not a formula. Not a franchise. Just hard-earned wisdom about what *actually* helps and what unintentionally harms.

The goal was never control.

It was empowerment.

We wanted others to take their place at the table—to stand against this evil in ways that fit their community, their people, their capacity.

And it worked.

Today, the Freedom Railroad is real.

It isn't defined by bunk beds or programs on paper. It's defined by people—living, breathing communities who know how to respond when someone calls for help. We've seen Jonah advocates serve alongside partners like Justice Ministries to help women from Michigan to North Carolina, and all across Washington State. Jonah's advocates have taken a baseball program to Zambia, Africa (Yes! Can you believe it??) with kids traveling to be coaches! It's taken root in high schools across Spokane, partnered with agencies across the U.S, like Underground Railroad and shared resources with other anti-trafficking agencies like Mirror Ministries or Pure Hope.

Building relationships. For those that have stayed alongside The Jonah Project, they know this was never about empire-building.

It has always been about building *paths to freedom*.

And the Freedom Railroad?
It's one of the strongest we've ever built.

Passage 21 — An Offering in the Sun

There was a moment—one of those gut-check crossroads—when I was offered a job pastoring at another church.

It came with a steady paycheck. A bigger platform. The pitch was simple: I could keep doing Jonah, but with more support behind me. More income meant my family could stop relying so heavily on food banks or EBT cards. Maybe finally breathe a little. Maybe give my kids some of the things I couldn't before.

The offer even came with a promise. This new church would support Jonah financially—on paper—to a higher degree than what we were used to.

But it also meant splitting my focus.

Leaving the frontline, at least in part.
A different flock.
A different calling.

I wrestled with it hard.

I had mouths to feed. A marriage to protect. And a mission that was growing beyond my capacity. I didn't want to abandon what God had entrusted to us—but I also didn't want to keep asking my wife and sons to carry the weight of my calling.

That same week, I walked into a church parking lot and saw one of the women from our ministry. A house-mom in fact.

It was hot outside. The sun was beating down. She was setting up tables, organizing donated shoes for sale. Sweat ran down her face, but her hands were steady as she lined them up—pair by pair—raising money for Jonah.

My instinct was to stop it.

To walk over, thank her, and tell her she didn't need to do this. I was about to—when a friend standing beside me said something I'll never forget.

"If you stop her, you're robbing her of her offering."

It hit me like a freight train.

She wasn't doing this because we asked her to. She wasn't doing it because she felt sorry for me or the Project. She was doing it because God had put something on her heart. Because this was her act of worship. Her way of saying, *I believe in what God is doing here.*

And in that moment, I realized something sacred.

Just because the road was hard didn't mean it was broken.

Sometimes the struggle was the altar.
Sometimes obedience looked like staying when you had every reason to go.

I turned down the job.

Not because I didn't want to provide better for my family—but because I trusted that God was still building something here. That He wasn't just inviting others to bring their offering.

He was asking me to bring mine.

Passage 22 — The Business of Ministry

As Jonah grew, other opportunities began to appear.

Not just opportunities to help—but opportunities to profit.

There were invitations to travel and speak. Requests to turn parts of the work into books, courses, or packaged programs. Doors that, on paper, looked like provision. Platforms that promised sustainability. Income. Stability.

And some of those opportunities were real. Legitimate. Well-intended.

But there was always a problem.

If I was on a stage, I wasn't answering the phone.
If I was doing news interviews, I wasn't doing relocations.
If I was building a brand, someone else would have to carry the weight when a call came in at two in the morning.

And at that time, there *was no someone else.*

There were moments—real ones—when choosing the "wise" option would have meant leaving a gap where rescue and relocation actually happened. Where a child or woman needed a body in a car, not a voice on a microphone.

So we stayed.

Not because we didn't believe in sharing the story—but because the story was still happening, and it needed hands more than headlines.

That choice came with a cost.

We lost donors because we wouldn't require conversion in exchange for care. We lost supporters who wanted visible outcomes, spiritual metrics, or public testimonies. Some couldn't understand why we wouldn't make church attendance or belief a condition for help.

Others wanted Jonah to become something scalable and profitable—something that could generate income, expand faster, and attract larger funding streams.

But we couldn't do it.

Because once you attach leverage to love, it stops being love.

We also lost friends. People who believed deeply in the cause—but not in the refusal to monetize it. People who thought we were wasting momentum. Leaving money on the table. Squandering opportunity.

I wish I could say that navigating those moments required great strategic wisdom or careful planning.

It didn't.

At my best, all I could do was listen.

Listen for God's voice.
Listen for when to move and when to stay.
Listen for what *not* to touch, even when it looks like provision.

There were seasons when obedience didn't feel heroic. It felt quiet. Risky. Lonely. Like choosing to trust a promise without knowing how it would be kept.

But I knew this much:

God had a plan.

Not for Jonah—we were just the vehicle. No, God had a much bigger plan and it was for the people Jonah existed to serve.

So we kept choosing presence over profit. Faithfulness over expansion. Relationship over transaction.

Not because it was easy.
Not because it was smart by worldly standards.

But because the work was never ours to monetize.

It was His to sustain.

And somehow—again and again—He did.

Passage 23 — A Mother's Plea

Some rescues don't begin with a phone call or a counselor referral. Sometimes they begin with a whisper.

A quiet, almost embarrassed voice from someone who doesn't want to ask—but knows they have to.

That's how this one began.

The woman who came to me that day wasn't a stranger. She was a friend. In fact, she'd known me before I knew God. Since my family first moved to Washington in 2008, she'd been part of our lives—someone who had seen our journey from both the outside and the inside. Her heart was always tender, always fierce for her family.

But this day was different.

Her shoulders were heavy. Her voice cracked when she said, "Aaron, I hate asking you… but I don't know what else to do."

Her daughter was trapped.

She was living with a biker who was also the father of her baby. The man wasn't just controlling—he was dangerous. He kept them locked away in an apartment, refusing to let them leave. It wasn't constant violence, but it didn't need to be. Control was enough. Fear hung in the air, always present, always threatening.

Her daughter wanted out.
But she wouldn't leave without her baby.

And the truth was, it wasn't safe for either of them.

Like most situations, this one required planning.

Real planning.

We briefed the team. We gathered what information we could about the location—entrances, exits, the layout of the neighborhood. In Spokane, many homes have alleys behind them. In Eastern Washington, basements are common, which means a lot can happen out of sight.

This particular apartment complex had a nearby neighbor who was known to be aggressive—someone with a military background, possibly volatile. So we assessed risk carefully. We built a threat picture based on what we knew and tried not to speculate about what we didn't.

We activated the team and began the careful work of determining how to extract both mother and baby safely.

When a baby is involved, mistakes aren't an option.

No chaos.
No rushing.

And there's an important difference here. In trafficking situations, it's sometimes possible to talk a pimp into letting a girl go. In domestic situations, anything can happen. Control is personal. Pride is involved. The risk profile changes completely.

We got them out.

I won't share details about the extraction itself, where they went, or how things unfolded afterward. In stories like this, anonymity isn't just courtesy—it's protection.

But I will say this.

That moment—when a mother came to us not just on behalf of her daughter, but her grandchild—reminded me again why this work mattered. Why advocacy wasn't optional. Why showing up wasn't just about rescue, but about standing in the gap long enough for someone else to breathe again.

Today, that woman and her child are living a life of their choosing. They're making free choices. My friend and I still talk whenever we can, and she remains as fiercely loving toward her family as she ever was.

God heard the cry of two mothers.

And He met them both with mercy.

Jonah was simply allowed, in that moment, to be a vehicle for His grace.

Passage 24 — When It Doesn't Get Easier

There's a quiet assumption people make about work like this.

That once awareness spreads, things get easier.
That once partnerships form, the burden lightens.
That once a city names a problem, the weight begins to lift.

That isn't how it works.

Sometimes the opposite happens.

As Jonah matured, as the work became more visible, we didn't feel less strain—we felt more. Not because the work was failing, but because the illusion that someone else would eventually take it over slowly disappeared.

Spokane, as a city, never fully rose to the occasion.

There were moments of interest. Seasons of attention. Resolutions passed. Panels formed. Headlines written. But sustained ownership—the kind that costs something—never quite arrived. The work remained hard, messy, and largely unseen.

Over time, we watched people fade out.

Friends in law enforcement transferred, retired, or burned out. Advocates from other organizations stepped back when the emotional cost became too high. Anti-trafficking initiatives that once felt urgent quietly dissolved when funding dried up or leadership changed.

None of this came from bad intentions.

It came from exhaustion.

This work asks people to look at things they'd rather not see, to sit with pain they can't fix, and to stay present long after the adrenaline wears off. For many, that's not sustainable forever—and that truth has to be honored.

But it can still be disheartening.

Especially when the need doesn't slow down.

Calls still come.
Stories still surface.
Kids still fall through cracks that were never fully closed.

There were moments when it felt like we were running uphill while the ground kept shifting beneath us. Moments when it would have been easier to scale back, narrow the focus, or redefine success in ways that hurt less.

But the people we served didn't get that option.

Trauma doesn't pause because systems are tired. Exploitation doesn't wait for better funding cycles. And survivors don't stop needing advocates just because the work has lost its momentum in public conversation.

That reality forced a question we couldn't avoid:

What do you do when the work remains necessary, but the helpers begin to disappear?

For Jonah, the answer was never to force endurance.

We learned to let people go with blessing. To honor seasons. To resist the temptation to guilt others into staying. This work cannot be sustained through pressure. Only through calling.

At the same time, we had to confront a harder truth: if we stayed, it would not be because the work became easier or more rewarding. It would be because God's heart had not changed—even when circumstances did.

That distinction mattered.

Because staying out of obligation breeds resentment. Staying out of fear breeds burnout. But staying out of faith—quiet, uncelebrated faith—does something different. It anchors you to something deeper than outcomes.

This was not the season for expansion.
It was the season for endurance.

For refining why we were here in the first place. For remembering that Jonah was never meant to carry the entire weight of this issue, but it was meant to carry *its* part faithfully.

Not everyone is called to this.

But some are.

And learning the difference—without judgment, without pride—became one of the most important lessons of all.

Passage 25 — Seeds planted…

There comes a moment in any work that begins with urgency when a different kind of faith is required.

At first, faith looks like stepping in—saying yes when no one else will. It looks like filling gaps, taking calls, showing up early and staying late. It looks like carrying weight because there's no one else to carry it yet.

But if the work is real—if it's meant to last longer than one season—faith eventually has to look like something else.

It has to look like letting go.

I ran Jonah from its founding until 2018–2019. Those early years required a particular posture—speed, responsiveness, risk tolerance, and a willingness to live in constant disruption. Rescue was still necessary. Advocacy was being invented in real time. Systems didn't exist yet, so improvisation did.

But the work was changing.

I'd spent so much time in prayer and was as certain as ever that one day the Project would need someone else to step up and lead - not just because of the emotional and physical toll - but out of skillset and to adapt to the mission.

Jonah no longer needed a founder who could sprint indefinitely. It needed leadership that could *stay*. Leadership that could build depth instead of momentum. Care instead of urgency. Structure instead of reaction.

That leadership came through Bindi.

And alongside her, Michelina.

They were, and are, the most gifted child advocates I have ever worked with. I believe many folks in ministry or in local law enforcement would say the same.

But the shift wasn't clean. It never is. Ministry handoffs rarely look heroic or orderly. There were hard conversations, growing pains, and moments of uncertainty. But what mattered was this: Jonah didn't collapse when leadership changed.

It clarified.

Under Bindi's leadership, advocacy deepened. The work moved further into aftercare, long-term support, and survivor-centered decision-making. The goal was no longer simply to respond to crisis, but to walk with people over time—sometimes for years.

Michelina emerged as a powerhouse advocate and eventually a lead advocate, working shoulder-to-shoulder with Bindi. Together, they strengthened what Jonah had always been moving toward: care that was trauma-informed, leverage-free, and rooted in dignity.

Advocacy expanded beyond individual cases into education. Teaching teachers. Training nurses. Equipping counselors. Planting seeds that would grow long after a single interaction ended. The Freedom Railroad matured, not as a brand, but as a living network of people who knew how to show up without controlling outcomes.

Some of the hardest conversations during this transition weren't logistical—they were relational.

There were people who had come to see me as an oracle of sorts. Not intentionally, and not maliciously—but through years of crisis, decisions, and visible leadership, they had begun to associate stability with my presence. When they heard I was stepping back, fear surfaced quickly.

What if everything changes?
What if what we've invested in falters?
What if the heart of Jonah gets lost?

Looking back now, I can see that fear for what it was. Not resistance. Not distrust. But the love was mixed with anxiety. People were afraid of losing a grip on something that mattered deeply to them.

And that fear revealed something important to me.

After all these years, I understand more clearly why God called me into this work in the first place. It wasn't just because of my rescue skills. Or my sermons. Or my willingness to speak publicly about hard things. It wasn't even my stubbornness or the tenacity with which I loved these kids.

It was because I would always fight to ensure this work remained *God's will being done*—not mine.

That was the true stewardship The Project needed from me.

And precisely why being able to let go mattered. It's part of the example we must set that this thing we have all birthed together does not belong *to us*.

It was not a surprise to me that Jonah survived the transition.

Or that it became more itself.

I'd been having these conversations with God from the start..

Jonah could never survive if it was built around my personality, my skill set, or my availability. It was built around a conviction—that freedom is worth protecting and that people heal best when they are not managed, but loved. That was the project. That was the experiment… Now I would see it work again without me needing to be the torch-bearer.

Stepping back didn't mean stepping away from that conviction. It meant trusting that God could steward it through Bindi and Michelina, and one day others, just as faithfully as He had through me.

Holding too tightly would have turned stewardship into control.

And control has no place in healing.

Jonah didn't need to revolve around one voice or one style of leadership. It needed to grow roots deep enough to withstand change. The fact that it did—that it continues to serve, advocate, and walk with hundreds, now thousands, of women and children—is not an accident.

It's evidence.

Evidence that the work was never about building something that lasted forever, but about building people who could carry the work forward.

Letting Jonah outgrow me was not the end of my calling.

It's proof that the calling is real.

Passage 26 — The Great Equalizer

There were moments when I was keenly aware of how unqualified I looked on paper.

I didn't have letters after my name. No formal credentials in social work or criminal justice. I wasn't trained in academia or shaped by institutions that usually get invited into rooms where decisions are made. And yet, somehow, those doors kept opening.

Meetings with the county sheriff.
Teaching sessions at WSU.
Conversations with other nonprofits trying to understand how we were doing what we were doing.

I remember speaking at Gonzaga University to a paid and sold-out crowd, and I remember the way I felt looking in the program that day and seeing a P.H.D. next to every single name but mine.

But we got funding and one of our best relo agents from that gathering.

Not because we had the cleanest model—but because the work was real.

Another moment stands out.

I was sitting in a meeting with an FBI advocate—a liaison responsible for placing kids and evaluating safe housing options. She was interested in Jonah's home, but I could tell she was measuring us carefully. We were faith-based. That alone made her cautious. She needed to know whether we'd be rigid, conditional, or hard to work with.

Midway through our conversation, my phone rang.

A relocation call.

I answered it.

Right there in the meeting.

I didn't dramatize it. I didn't explain much. I just took the call, gathered what I needed, and made arrangements. When I hung up, the tone in the room had changed.

Legitimacy doesn't always come from resumes.
Sometimes it comes from readiness.

She didn't say much at that moment—but later, it became clear she'd seen what she needed to see. This wasn't a theory. It was practice. The work wasn't something we talked about—it was something we did.

By far, though, the most fruitful relationships we ever developed were with our local DHS agents.

Two in particular—I'll call them Blane and Sabrina—are still close friends to Bindi and me to this day.

I didn't walk into that Homeland Security meeting alone.

Nicole Bishop—my assistant at the time, who would later serve on the Spokane Human Rights Commission herself—was with me that day. We had been called into the DHS office to explain who we were and what we were doing in Spokane. They were feeling us out too. Trying to understand if we were safe to work with. If we understood the gravity of the work. If our faith would complicate collaboration.

We talked about resources—what we had and what we didn't. We talked about care. About safety. About the long road of healing these kids would walk.

And slowly, the conversation shifted.

It moved from logistics to philosophy.
From policy to people.

We found ourselves talking openly with two federal agents about the power of relationship in healing. About trust. About presence. About how kids who've been trafficked don't need more systems—they need consistency.

Eventually, faith entered the conversation—not as a dividing line, but as common ground. Not doctrine, but passion. A shared longing to see trafficking in this area end.

We bonded there.

Not because we checked the same boxes—but because we cared about the same kids.

When we walked out of that meeting, Nicole was stunned. She looked at me and said she couldn't believe what had just happened—that we had just sat across the table from two federal agents and talked openly about faith, love, and hope as essential elements of healing.

That relationship grew. It deepened. And it changed the work.

I'm reminded by now former federal agent and friend, Blane, of the first time Jonah and DHS spoke at an event together - at St. Peter's in Spokane. When I learned that DHS would be there that day and we were the "opening act" I recall wondering why we were even needed. Surely we were small potatoes compared to whatever they would have to offer.

We greeted each other, me, Bindi and the two DHS agents - and then I rose to speak. I talked to those gathered for about 20 minutes and then sat back down absolutely sure I was about to really look silly in front of the real experts. As the first agent rose to speak he said, "I'd like to start off by saying thank you to Aaron - and The Jonah Project for their work - that was the most accurate, detailed and passionate dissertation on child trafficking I've heard in over 20 years on this job."

I still feel that God himself gave our team an added aura of public legitimacy from the statement - and I'll always be thankful that it is indeed God, not man, who qualifies us to do good works.

Gone are the days when Jonah has to step into rescues the way we once did. Now, when a situation escalates, Bindi can call our DHS partners—and they handle that part of the work. She walks alongside them, advocating for care, ensuring the survivor isn't lost once the crisis passes.

That didn't happen because we demanded a seat at the table.

It happened because we showed up faithfully—again and again—long before anyone was watching.

God has a way of qualifying people the world overlooks.

Not by credentials.
Not by titles.
But by faithfulness in motion.

God made a way.

He is the great equalizer.

Doors opened not because we insisted we belonged there—but because the work made room for us.

And once inside, the work kept speaking for itself.

Passage 27 — Ordinary Miracles

If you asked me early on what success looked like, I probably would have answered with numbers.

Rescues completed.
Calls answered.
Beds filled.
Crises interrupted.

Those things mattered. They still do. But they were never the point.

The truest measure of this work didn't reveal itself in emergencies. It showed up quietly, years later, in moments no one would ever think to count.

Wedding invitations.

Graduation announcements.

Text messages that simply said, *"Hey... I was thinking about you today."*

These were the moments that stopped me in my tracks—not because they were dramatic, but because they were ordinary. And for many of the kids we served, ordinary once felt impossible.

Some of the young people who came through Jonah were labeled unsalvageable long before we met them. Too traumatized. Too unstable. Too far gone. Systems had already written them off, quietly and efficiently.

But time has a way of telling the truth.

Today, Bindi and Michelina receive invitations to weddings where survivors stand at the altar, steady and joyful. We see pictures of graduations—caps crooked, smiles wide. We hear about jobs, apartments, babies, ordinary frustrations, ordinary hopes.

Lives.

Not perfect ones. But real ones.

What strikes me most is how rarely these moments are framed as miracles by the people living them. They don't see themselves as success stories. They see themselves as people who were given space to grow, room to fail, and permission to keep going.

That's what advocacy looks like in the long run.

It doesn't produce headlines.
It produces birthdays.
Anniversaries.
School mornings.
Quiet nights where no one is afraid to sleep.

There's a particular kind of joy in watching someone live a life that no longer revolves around survival. In seeing them choose partners carefully. Build families intentionally. Set boundaries. Laugh freely.

It's not flashy.

But it's sacred.

These moments remind me that the work didn't end when the crisis passed. It didn't even end when Jonah changed leadership or focus. It continued—inside people—long after the need for us faded into the background of their lives.

And that's exactly how it should be.

We were never meant to be the center of anyone's story. We were meant to walk alongside them until they no longer needed us in that way.

When survivors invite us into their ordinary joy, it's not because we saved them. It's because we stayed long enough for them to save themselves.

That's the kind of legacy you can't manufacture.

You can't program it.
You can't rush it.
And you certainly can't control it.

You can only plant faithfully and trust God with the growth.

Jonah's story is woven now into hundreds—soon thousands—of other stories. Not as a chapter they revisit, but as a foundation they've built upon.

And when I see that—when I watch people living lives that once seemed unreachable—I'm reminded that the most powerful miracles are rarely the ones that interrupt life.

They're the ones that allow life to finally begin.

Passage 28 — Staying

There is a difference between hope and illusion.

Illusion tells you that if you work hard enough, speak clearly enough, love fiercely enough, the systems around you will eventually rise to meet the need. That cities will catch up. That institutions will adjust. That momentum, once gained, will carry itself.

Hope knows better.

Hope knows that the work may remain difficult. That attention will drift. That resources will thin. That people—good people—will step away when the cost becomes too high for the season they're in.

There were moments of progress. Awareness campaigns. Public conversations. Resolutions passed. But sustained ownership—the kind that actually changes outcomes—never truly took hold. What did happen instead was quieter and harder to measure: pressure.

Not public pressure.
Relational pressure.
Moral pressure.

Seeds planted through Jonah forced other institutions to look at their own gaps. Emergency rooms became better equipped to recognize signs of trafficking—not because the city mandated it, but because Jonah had a board member embedded in the hospital system who refused to let the issue stay theoretical. After hundreds of survivors passed through our care, word spread. Not through marketing, but through results.

This is what trust looks like with institutions: earned slowly, resisted fiercely.

Trust is hard with survivors.
It is just as hard—sometimes harder—with systems.

Complacency is powerful. Funding structures reward appearance more than impact. And competition, even in the nonprofit world, often masquerades as concern.

I remember when we launched one of the first trafficking-awareness billboards in the city. It carried a resource phone number that led to direct help. Almost immediately, a large social services organization erected a billboard right next to it—with their own number.

The problem was simple: their number didn't offer direct help.

It routed callers through a national messaging system, with possible referrals for resources.. But the billboard wasn't about helping victims. It was about funding. About competition for what the nonprofit community often sees as a finite amount of resource. A slice of a pie. And of course - making sure *they* were seen as the organization responding to the problem.

Meanwhile, Jonah was literally housing the kids those same offices sent away. Sharing safe homes with the FBI. Answering phones at all hours. Doing the work no one wanted to fund for no pay - because it was too risky, too relational, and too hard to scale.

That tension never really went away. Over time, we watched people burn out.

Law enforcement partners transferred or retired. Friends in other anti-trafficking organizations stepped back when the emotional toll became too high. City initiatives stalled once the headlines faded. Programs dissolved quietly when grants ended or leadership changed.

None of that surprised God.

And none of it changed His heart.

It did, however, underscore for me the truth that we must be about Freedom always - and that one day Jonah might end or we will be called to something else - but whatever that is, it too will be *about Freedom.*

We were taught about faithfulness in a specific place, for a specific time, with the people God has placed in front of you—even when the system around you resists change.

Jonah was necessarily meant to be permanent.

But it was meant to be disruptive!

Disruptive to programmatic thinking.
Disruptive to leverage-based care.
Disruptive to the idea that survivors should be grateful for scraps.

The advocates who poured themselves into this work will not always be Jonah advocates. They will become teachers, counselors, parents, nurses, administrators—carrying with them a different standard for what care should look like. The heartbeat of this work will follow them into spaces Jonah may never enter directly.

The survivors we walked with will go on to live lives that no longer include us at all. And that is not loss. That is success. Their healing was never meant to orbit around Jonah. It was meant to free them.

Even now, the work looks different than it once did.

Rescue and relocation are no longer the center of what Jonah does.
Advocacy has deepened and is the core.
Systems that once resisted have been forced—slowly, unevenly—to do better.

Still, the need remains.

That tension—between impact and incompletion—can be discouraging if you expect resolution.

But God does not measure faithfulness by completion.

He measures it by obedience.

Jonah will survive as long as God needs this particular group of people, in this particular place, for this particular time. And when that season ends, the light will not go out.

It will simply move.

Because the work was never about an organization.

It was about presence in the dark.
And staying faithfully—long enough to force the light in.

Passage 29 — Lessons

By now, you'll see I was honest with you when I said this wasn't just my story, but a story I am simply telling. Its lives intertwined instead of string attached. And each of these Passages shares a lesson or two – or three. But there is a particular lesson I want to share with you that will always resonate... So if you'll be patient with me just awhile longer, I'll attempt to do it justice.

A good friend of mine, a brother really – Tim Kuhn, approached me one night after a small gathering. He had an idea.

Tim is an unassuming guy and when he has something to share – I always want to hear it. And truth be told, I'd been praying for more ideas, more involvement and engagement in that season – especially from the men in the community.

As he pulled me aside he began to share his inspiration for serving the women and girls we were housing in Lighthouse (teen home) and Hearthouse (women's home). This kind of darkness attacks the spirit and soul he noted – and the most productive spiritual warfare he counseled – was moving directly opposite the darkness... these people had all had their value and dignity assaulted and eroded. We needed to do something special and extraordinary to help them gain it back.

So Tim planned a formal dinner to honor the ladies and girls and their advocates who are also women. It wasn't just any dinner either. He recruited each of the male volunteers to dress up and wait tables, cook an amazing meal, and there was Tim directing traffic with a passion. He had found a place for each of us guys to pitch in – and designed table pieces – and a single yellow rose for each gal that walked through the door, the 12 year old and the 42 year old and every lady in between.

The ladies as the guests of honor were waited on hand and foot – a girl broke down crying saying she'd always wanted a rose. Another stood and headed to the front of the room where she began telling the men why it was so important to her and the other ladies that we'd wanted to show they were important and wonderful. And they noticed everything. I saw the men beaming with pride as the women and kids praised their efforts and I saw the kids so excited to be with all the grown up ladies. *It was church!*

The advocates got to mix some of the survivors they'd not met and our clients, those survivors, got to just be themselves for a night – safe and part of the community. Like all of our events, this was done with volunteers and good intentions – and God's blessing.

So many still talk about that night. And I learned a lot of lessons from it. The power of a dinner – not to raise money but to raise spirits. Many of us, just like the men before Tim rallied us, can feel impotent when it comes to serving someone we don't know or maybe, don't understand.

That's okay.

How we win is to let Love have it's way. We stick our boots in the ground, take aim, and we push back, *hard*, against the dark.

Passage 30 — When Jonah Becomes a Memory

Every work that matters eventually reaches a quiet question.

Not *Did it succeed? Did it last?*

But Did it obey?

Jonah was never meant to live forever.

That's not resignation. It's theology.

God does not build monuments. He builds people. He does not preserve organizations for their own sake. He sends them, uses them, and—when the season is complete—allows them to become stories carried forward in living hearts.

One day, Jonah will become a memory.

Not because the need ended.
Not because the work failed.
But because seasons change, and God is not afraid of endings.

When that day comes, there will be no grand announcement. No countdown. No curtain call. The phones will stop ringing as often. The meetings will thin. The work will quietly move elsewhere—into classrooms, hospitals, homes, churches, city offices, and ordinary conversations.

And that will be enough.

Because by then, Jonah's heartbeat will no longer belong to Jonah.

It will live in advocates who learned how to show up without leverage, who learned how to listen without fixing, who learned how to stay present without needing credit. It will live in teachers who see differently now. In nurses who ask better questions. In counselors who refuse to rush healing. In parents who open their homes when the answer would be easier.

It will live in survivors who no longer need us.

That may be the hardest truth to accept—and the most beautiful.

We don't stay in their lives forever. We aren't meant to. Healing that still requires us at the center is not healing at all. The goal was always freedom. And freedom, by definition, moves on.

Some of the kids who once slept under our roofs now invite us to weddings. Some who once needed rides to appointments now send graduation photos. Some who once couldn't imagine tomorrow now complain about jobs, marriages, kids, and bills—ordinary frustrations that would have felt like miracles once.

And they are.

Those moments will never be recorded in annual reports. They won't be credited to Jonah in any official way. And that's right. The work was never about recognition. It was about restoring people to lives so full that the rescue fades into the background.

Even now, Spokane is still imperfect.

Systems still resist change. Funding still follows visibility more than impact. People still burn out. Evil still adapts. Darkness still finds new places to hide.

But God's heart has not changed.

He is still seeking the lost.
Still drawing near to the broken.
Still asking ordinary people to carry light into dark places—not forever, but faithfully.

Jonah existed because there was a gap.

And when the gap closes—or shifts, or moves—God will raise up others. He always does.

The light doesn't disappear when one lamp goes out.

It spreads.

So if Jonah becomes a memory, let it be this kind of memory:

Not a brand.
Not a building.
Not a program.

But a season when people chose presence over safety, obedience over outcomes, and love without leverage in a world addicted to control.

That is enough.

That has always been enough.

And wherever the light goes next, God will already be there—waiting, calling, and staying.

> *"If you hear the dogs, keep going.*
> *If you see the torches in the woods, keep going.*
> *If there's shouting after you, keep going.*
> *Don't ever stop. Keep going.*
> *If you want a taste of freedom, keep going."*
> **— Harriet Tubman**

An Open Letter:
To Those That Wish to Love Fiercely

If you are still here, still reading, still holding the weight of these stories—this part is for you.

Because anyone who walks long enough alongside pain eventually carries it. Anyone who chooses to see what others turn away from will feel it settle into their bones. And anyone who dares to love the broken without leverage will discover just how costly that love can be.

So before anything else, hear this clearly: **take care of yourself.** Rest when you can. Speak when you're weary. Let others carry you when the load becomes too heavy. This work will demand your heart, freely given. Trust God with the outcomes you cannot control. He was never asking you to be the Savior—only to walk faithfully with Jesus.

The truth is, this path is not new.

When the early Christian church was most threatened—when believers were fed to lions in Roman arenas, when faith meant secrecy and survival— we understood something essential about the heart of God. Even then, we knew He was not kidding when He said, *"Hinder not the children unto Me."*

In those early days, followers of Jesus would slip out under the cover of night. They would move quietly through the city streets heading outside the city walls at times, past burning refuse piles and smoldering trash heaps, listening.

Listening for the cries of babies.

The unwashed and unwanted babies—the boy with the club foot, the girl with the cleft palate, children conceived in violence, children deemed inconvenient— thrown away to die. And the church went looking for them. Digging through ash and waste, risking exposure, persecution, and death—

not because they had resources, or plans, or systems in place, but because they had mercy.

The broken, saving the broken, with nothing to offer but mercy… and a place to belong.

God's heart has never changed.

But perhaps we have?

Somewhere along the way, we became more comfortable with "boundaries". With systems that keep suffering orderly. With compassion that stays clean. We learned how to feel concern without cost, outrage without involvement, and sympathy rather than empathy

So the question still stands.

Are we willing to seek and save the lost?

Will we get dirty again?
Will we dig where it smells like smoke and refuse?
Will we look for the child who has been thrown away?
Will we open our homes, our schedules, our lives?
Will we say *yes*—not knowing where the road will lead?

Because that was the question God asked me, long before Jonah had a name.

Would you?

For those who answer yes, understand this: you may find yourself walking paths you never asked for, in places you never imagined. You will encounter heartbreak you cannot fix and stories you cannot forget. There will be moments when the cost feels unbearable.

But His love will guide you every step of the way.

And something else will happen too—something quiet, something holy. Your love will grow. With every child brought home. With every life seen as worthy. With every act of mercy offered freely, without strings.

This is how light moves through darkness.
Not loudly.
Not efficiently.
But faithfully.

If you are still here—still willing—may God give you courage, wisdom, rest, and grace in equal measure.

And may you never forget: Love still wins!

A FEW TESTIMONIES...

"Jonah Project has been an amazing organization to work with. They work tirelessly to meet students with their needs and where they are at. I have had two students that I work with housed with Jonah Project. Not only did Jonah Project house these vulnerable youth, but went above and beyond. Jonah Project helped get these students mental health services, substance abuse counseling, clothing, mentors and appropriate school placements. Their communication with me has always been excellent, and we have worked together every step of the way to get these high risk kiddos to a stable spot. I have enjoyed working with each and every staff that I have met through the Jonah Project!"
-Danielle Duffey
HEART Specialist - N.C. high school

"My daughter had basically been missing for 3 1/2 years and we finally were able to locate her at a shelter (out of state)... My son connected with The Jonah Project and we were walked through a rescue by Bindi Tilbury...Bindi and JP have walked side by side with us ever since. I don't know how we would have gotten through this without the support and care my daughter received from this organization."
"L"
Mom of a Trafficking Survivor

"Just think to yourself, who would go out of there way with no financial payoff or benefit, or even leave the country to and travel thousands of miles away...to save a young mother with children? If anyone was gonna stand by me it was Jonah."
"Pearl"
Teen Trafficking Survivor - 17

"Jesus didn't say, "bring the world to us", but rather, "go into all the world" (Mark 16:15). The Jonah Project is a shining example of this commission, going into the dark and sad places to rescue the broken and hurting. Both in our community here in Spokane and also on a broader level, working with Homeland Security and other public and government officials, they strive to show the love of Christ and what freedom can truly look like. The unconditional love they show to those they reach out to and rescue from human trafficking is a dangerous love; a love that extends to places most of us aren't willing to go. This is why we at Life Center Church support The Jonah Project, because God calls us to partner together to reach those who need rescuing and above all need Jesus. The Jonah Project doesn't just preach the gospel, they live it out boldly, and who wouldn't want to be a part of that? We are excited about what God is doing through The Jonah Project and excited about our partnership with them."

-Krista Lack
Spokane Serving Director - LIFE CENTER

"We love you guys! Thank you for showing us that someone really cares for us, and for showing us love like no one else. Its hard for us to leave! You really changed our lives."

"Beth & Dee"
Teen Trafficking Survivors - 17 & 16

"Yes my babies and I deserve to be treated better and will get better with my family, Just kept praying and having the lord with us everyday to keep strength and never giving up fighting for what's best and keeping us safe. I thank you and the Jonah family for helping us at this time. Again I couldn't thank you enough."

"Heather"
Teen Mom/Trauma Survivor - 18

"The Jonah Project is an organization that has provided me with various resources. The Jonah Project has donated many things to me when I was in a time of struggle...clothing, hygiene products, and food to name a few. JP has great advocates that have helped me with my needs, like getting me to appointments to providing mentoring... A time that sticks out to me was when an advocate helped me with my financial aid for college, or when an advocate took me to get a replacement of my social security card. Or when an advocate took me to my counselor's appointment. For me there is a specific advocate that makes sure I have everything I need. She is constantly checking in with me and providing emotional support. Having a caring, positive influence does make the difference. The Jonah Project is a special organization that has a lot to offer people in need. There is so much good that has been and will be done by the Jonah Project and I can testify to that."

"Janelle"
Teen Survivor 16

Appendix Notice & Reader Advisory

This appendix is included to provide transparency into the values and boundaries that supported the work described in this book. It is not a manual, training guide, or set of instructions for intervention.

Operational details related to rescue, relocation, security, and risk mitigation are intentionally omitted. The work described occurred within specific relationships, experience levels, and accountability structures that cannot be safely replicated without proper training and support.

This appendix documents responsibility—not instruction.

Protection of Survivors and Staff

All survivor names, identifying details, locations, and timelines have been altered or fictionalized to protect privacy and safety. These changes preserve dignity without altering the substance of the stories.

Names of Jonah Project members are used with consent.

What This Appendix Is—and Is Not

This appendix is:

A record of the guardrails that made compassion sustainable

A reflection of trauma-informed principles learned through experience

Context for why certain boundaries existed

This appendix is not:

A rescue handbook or procedural guide

A model to be copied or scaled without context

An endorsement of independent or unsupervised action

Compassion without structure creates risk.

A Note on Safety and Intervention

Human trafficking involves significant danger and complexity. Untrained intervention can escalate harm or compromise long-term safety.

If you believe someone is in immediate danger, contact local emergency services or a trained, established organization equipped to respond appropriately. The Jonah Project never operated in isolation, and no individual should attempt to do so.

RESOURCE BINDER

The Jonah Project   RESCUE LINE: 509-655-7886   www.jonahproject.org

A LETTER FROM THE FOUNDER

September 11, 2017

Dear Friend,

Sex trafficking is slavery, pure and simple. It isn't prostitution; it isn't a lifestyle choice. That part is not complex.

What isn't so simple is how we got here. Or where we're going. In fact, sometimes we find ourselves grasping at straws or feeling overwhelmed just trying to figure out what to do and where to go for help, right now.

Maybe when you first heard about sex-slavery you didn't believe something like this could be real. Maybe you were so appalled at the numbers or victim's testimonies that you became angry...but then you began to become numb. Maybe you hoped that our law enforcement agencies had task forces raiding houses and rescuing victims every day, or that our city had funded a comprehensive plan to address the issues...and then you realized there are very little resources and very little volunteers and very little awareness. And that hope began to fade...

But your heart still couldn't let the issue go.

Because fundamentally, this is about Freedom for us all. Freedom.

Its something beyond politics and religion, gender or culture. It is the thing many of us say we would die for. And it is being denied to so many of our women and children.

There are more slaves now than at any other time in human history. The slave trade is the second fastest growing criminal industry in the world. Every day in our schools, our neighborhoods, and across this nation our children are being targeted and preyed upon. Some have begun to see themselves without worth or value. Many are losing hope that we will ever bring them home. And even more have been lost forever...

It is now more than ever we must rise up and be a voice for those that have none. Now more than ever, to be the hands and feet of our Faith. In every time and every season freedom has ever been threatened in this nation's history, it has required those not directly affected by the problem to walk alongside those who are. For sympathetic minds to make way for empathetic voices, and for our love for one another to override our baser instincts.

To walk in the freedom which we believe is the birthright of us all.

Will you join hands and walk with us?

Yours in Him,

A. P. Tilbury

The Jonah Project　　　RESCUE LINE: 509-655-7886　　　www.jonahproject.org

TABLE OF CONTENTS

SECTION TITLE	PAGE NUMBER
Section 1: Sex Trafficking 101	1
Section 2: Spokane and Human Trafficking	2
Section 3: Recognizing & Reporting Human Trafficking	5
- Tactics - Changes in Behavior - Basic Stages of Grooming - Who to Report To	
Section 4: Our History	8
- Mission - What We Do	
Section 5: Guiding Principle: Transparent Aftercare	10
- Understanding Trafficking Victims - Principles of Transparent Aftercare	
Section 6: Resource <=> Resident Sphere of Influence	12
Section 7: Interview & Assessment Info and Checklist	13
- Setting up the Interview - Developing Trust/Demonstrating Respect -Understanding Trauma	
-Under 18 Specific -Health	
*Section 8: Human Trafficking in a Health Care Setting	18
*Section 9: Sex Trafficking Power and Control Wheel	19
Section 10: Intake Protocol	20
Section 11: Emergency Assessment & Contact Info	21
Section 12: Alternate (written) Intake Questionnaire	22
Section 13: Housing Intake & Information Sheet	23
Section 14: Assessment Team Goals	24
Section 15: Volunteer Do's & Don'ts	25
Section 16: Core Resident & Volunteer Expectations	26
Section 17: Expectations & Responsibilities: House Leaders & Advocates	27
Section 18: Daily & Long Term Care Plans	28
Section 19: Stage 1 & 2 Care Plan	30
- Care Plan Stage 1 - Care Plan Stage 2 -Advocate Checklist A -Advocate Checklist B	
Rescue Line Information	34
*Lighthouse Info Sheet	35

* Coming soon to the online document

The Jonah Project   RESCUE LINE: 509-655-7886   www.jonahproject.org

1-SEX TRAFFICKING 101

WHAT: Sex trafficking is a form of modern-day slavery. Sex traffickers use violence, threats, lies, debt bondage, and other forms of coercion to compel adults and children to engage in commercial sex acts against their will (Polaris) for the trafficker's own profit. Trafficking has a harrowing effect on the mental, emotional, and physical well being of its victims.

WHO & WHERE: In America, about 325,000 in 2015; in Spokane, from 500 to 1500, and thousands in the "circuit" Spokane shares with Seattle, the Tri-Cities, Portland, Oregon and Idaho. Adult women make up the largest group of sex trafficking victims, followed by minor girls, although a growing number of men and boys are trafficked into the sex industry as well. Some sex-trafficking is highly visible, but many trafficking victims remain unseen, operating out of unmarked brothels in unsuspecting neighborhoods. Sex traffickers may also operate out of a variety of public locations, such as massage parlors, spas, hotels, and clubs.

WHEN: Women and girls are ensnared in sex trafficking in a variety of ways. Many are sold into trafficking by boyfriends, friends, neighbors, or even parents. It may occur through:

- Abduction
- Meet traffickers by responding to advertisements for modeling jobs or other legitimate work
- The promise of marriage, education, work or study abroad, and a better life
- Seeking the help of smugglers to enter the United States, then a debt-bondage ensues
- Being sold to traffickers by parents or an intimate partner

WHY: Sex trafficking can be extremely lucrative for the trafficker, especially in areas where opportunities for education and employment are limited. The second fastest growing crime in the world, it often accompanies drug sales due to its viable economics: you can sell a bag of drugs only once and must then buy more to resell, a girl can be sold 30 times or more every day without having to replenish the supply. For the victims who are held in this vicious cycle, the money, resources, and safe shelter they may have been promised is often never realized, and then they find themselves unable to escape.

HOW: Coercion, fraud, or force. The biggest tool any trafficker has is fear and violence. Victims are almost always subjected to harsh psychological and physical abuse, including repeated rape, to keep them submissive. According to one study, trafficking victims generally only see three ways of escape from their situation: 1) to become unprofitable because of trauma, emotional breakdown, or advanced pregnancy; 2) to be helped by a client; or 3) death. Sex trafficking victims experience various stages of degradation, physical and psychological torture. Victims are often deprived of food and sleep and are unable to move about freely. In order to keep women captive, victims are told their families and children will be harmed or murdered if they try to escape or tell anyone about their situation.

The Jonah Project   RESCUE LINE: 509-655-7886   www.jonahproject.org

2-SPOKANE & HUMAN TRAFFICKING

Spokane has become a part of a human trafficking "circuit" (both sex and labor). Many times those two areas intersect, and the same slaves are trafficked for both purposes. This circuit includes Seattle, Spokane and the Tri-Cities in Washington; Portland, Oregon; and Couer d'Alene, Post Falls, and Rathrum/Hayden in Idaho. Most statistics available are national; however, recent estimates by local government agencies estimate the number of trafficked girls in the area to be between 1000 and 1500, so there could be thousands in the "circuit" as a whole. We believe that even one is too many.

Evil and darkness do not discriminate; it could be the waitress pouring your coffee or the prom queen at an affluent high school. In Spokane we have found instances where gangs and even family members have "pimped out" their children and friends. It is believed that presently most of the trafficking in Spokane is smaller, loosely organized groups and gangs as opposed to what we see internationally where mafias typically run these operations at the highest levels. Many of the kids we serve will have been in situations where gangs, drugs, or violence were all part of daily life.

For more information on trafficking in Spokane, please visit the following links:

- http://www.seattletimes.com/seattle-news/study-sounds-alarm-on-human-trafficking-in-spokane-area/
- http://komonews.com/news/local/4-arrested-in-spokane-countys-first-reported-human-trafficking-case
- http://www.khq.com/story/18621179/court-documents-sex-slave-helps-bust-human-trafficking-ring-4-arrested
- http://www.huffingtonpost.com/dr-lois-lee/americas-child-sex-traffi_b_8118596.html
- http://www.krem.com/news/local/spokane-county/fbi-operation-hopes-to-decrease-sex-trafficking-in-spokane/188052892
- http://www.atg.wa.gov/news/news-releases/attorney-general-proposal-protect-human-trafficking-victims-passes-legislature
- https://www.youtube.com/watch?v=8M2TotAe2pg
- http://spokanecares.org/human-trafficking.php
- http://www.lcsnw.org/spokane/humantrafficking.html
- https://worldreliefspokane.org/anti-trafficking
- https://freetorunfoundation.org/2015/05/13/a-peak-into-sex-trafficking-in-the-pacific-northwest/
- http://bozzimedia.com/slavery-in-the-shadows/

The Jonah Project   RESCUE LINE: 509-655-7886   www.jonahproject.org

The street is no place for a kid
As they struggle to survive, kids often fall victim to predators ready to exploit the young and desperate

Staggering Statistics

63%
of underage sex trafficked victims say they had been advertised or sold online.

$200,000
The amount a pimp can make off each child they enslave per year. A pimp typically exploits 4-6 children.

15
The average number of times each child is sold for sex EACH DAY

2 Girls, 1 Boy
Of every three child sex trafficking victims, two are girls and one is a boy.

30 seconds
A child in the world is sold into slavery every thirty seconds.

1 in 3
Teens will be solicited or lured into slavery within 48 hours of being homeless.

1 in 5
Runaways were reportedly sex-trafficked. 74% had been in Foster Care.

11-12
The average age of child taken into sexual slavery.

7 Years
Average life span of a victim is reported to be 7 years (death by STD's, malnutrition, overdose, suicide, HIV, abuse, or attack are common).

3-RECOGNIZING & REPORTING HUMAN TRAFFICKING

The following organizations/websites are excellent sources of information to educate yourself about all aspects of human trafficking as well as provide you with tools to teach yourself how to identify potential human trafficking victims. Remember that it will take time and experience before many aspects of this field become second nature to you. In the mean time, keep your eyes open and engage!

- U.S. Department of Justice: www.justice.gov/humantrafficking
- Polaris: polarisproject.org
- NHTRC (National Human Trafficking Hotline): humantraffickinghotline.org
- Thorn: www.wearethorn.org

Traffickers often use isolation from family, friends, and the public to keep their victims in captivity. Limiting contact with outsiders and ensuring that any contact they do have is superficial in nature will prevent the victim from building social support networks in the community. As well, moving victims from place to place decreases the likelihood that the victim will form relationships and/or be recognized. The following are *some* indicators red flags:

- Does the person appear disconnected from family, friends, community organizations, and houses of worship?
- Has a child stopped attending school?
- Is the person disoriented or confused or showing signs of mental or physical abuse?
- Does the person have bruises in various stages of healing?
- Is the person fearful, timid, or submissive, or have trouble making eye contact?
- Is the person often in the company of someone to who he or she defers? Or someone who seems to be in control of the situation; e.g., where they go or who they talk to?
- Does the person appear to be coached on what to say?
- Does the person have freedom of movement? Can the person freely leave where they live?
- Is the person not in control of their time or money?
- Does the person dress overtly sexually or appear to dress/act in a way that is suggestive or manipulative?
- Are there any tattoos or branding marks on the person that are consistent with slavery/trafficking; i.e., scarring, men's names, crowns, or dollar signs incorporated into some other design?

The Jonah Project   RESCUE LINE: 509-655-7886   www.jonahproject.org

3-RECOGNIZING & REPORTING HUMAN TRAFFICKING

Grooming is when someone builds an emotional connection with a child to gain their trust for the purposes of sexual abuse, sexual exploitation or trafficking.

Children and young people can be groomed online or face-to-face, by a stranger or by someone they know - for example a family member, friend or professional.

Groomers may be male or female. They could be any age.

Many children and young people don't understand that they have been groomed or that what has happened is abuse.

Signs of grooming: The signs of grooming aren't always obvious and groomers will often go to great lengths not to be identified. If a child is being groomed they may:

- be very secretive, including about what they are doing online
- have older boyfriends or girlfriends
- go to unusual places to meet friends
- have new things such as clothes or mobile phones that they can't or won't explain
- have access to drugs and alcohol.

In older children, signs of grooming can easily be mistaken for 'normal' teenage behaviour, but you may notice unexplained changes in behaviour or personality, or inappropriate sexual behaviour for their age.

How common is grooming?

We don't know how common grooming is because often children don't tell anyone what is happening to them.

Children may not speak out because they are:

- Ashamed
- feeling guilty
- unaware that they're being abused
- believe they are in a relationship with a 'boyfriend' or 'girlfriend'.

Things you may notice: If you're worried that a child is being abused, watch out for any unusual behavior:

Withdrawn	Aggressive	Misses School	Alcohol
Suddenly Behaves Differently	Problems Sleeping	Changes in Eating Habits	Self-harm
Anxious	Eating Disorders	Obsessive Behavior	Thoughts About Suicide
Clingy	Wets the Bed	Nightmares	
Depressed	Soils Clothes	Drugs	
	Takes Risks		

SOURCE: https://www.nspcc.org.uk/preventing-abuse/child-abuse-and-neglect/grooming/

The Jonah Project   RESCUE LINE: 509-655-7886   www.jonahproject.org

BASIC STAGES OF
GROOMING
for sexual exploitation

(v) to prepare or train someone for a particular purpose or activity

END SLAVERY NOW

TARGETING A VICTIM
Traffickers target victims who have some noticeable vulnerability: emotional neediness, low self-confidence or economic stress.

GAINING TRUST & INFORMATION
Obtaining information about the victim is key. This can be done through casual conversations with the victim or with parents. Traffickers often mix well with other adults.

FILLING A NEED
The information gained allows the trafficker to fill a need in the victim's life, making the victim dependant on them in some way: buying gifts, being a friend, beginning a love relationship or buying soft drugs and alcohol.

❝ Up until this point they had never tried to touch me, they had not made me ever feel uncomfortable or ever feel unsafe or that they could harm me. ❞

ISOLATION
The trafficker creates times to be alone with the victim. The trafficker will also begin to have a major role in the victim's life and attempt to distance the victim from friends and family.

ABUSE BEGINS
The trafficker begins claiming that a service must be repaid whether money spent on cigarettes or drugs, car rides or mobile phones. In most cases, the trafficker demands sex as payment for such services.

❝ I trusted them, they were my friends as I saw it, until one night my main perpetrator raped me, quite brutally as well, in front of a number of people. ❞

MAINTAIN CONTROL

❝ Well if I didn't go out and see them they are going to get my mum and are going to rape her. ❞

In many cases, the trafficker maintains control of the victim through threats, violence, fear or blackmail.

3-RECOGNIZING & REPORTING HUMAN TRAFFICKING

WHO TO REPORT TO:

- **9-1-1**: If you think a crime is in progress or a victim is in immediate danger.
- **NTHRC (National Human Trafficking Hotline) at 1-888-373-7888**: for all instances you KNOW are human trafficking related.
- **Crime Check at 509-456-2233**: In all cases, when it is safe to do so, call and secure a report/case # for us to reference.
- **The Jonah Project Team**: In Spokane, we are currently the only qualified team doing rescue & relocation. The heart of our project, which is Shelter and Advocacy, helps us meet the needs of school counselors, local agencies, and of course, the victims in our area.

The Jonah Project   RESCUE LINE: 509-655-7886   www.jonahproject.org

4.1-OUR HISTORY

The Jonah Project started as a collaboration. A relationship. And we still operate that way today. From the pastor and school counselor to the women's service/agency or shelter that calls us for assistance, to the victims and survivors and advocates.. we are all one family. As Dr. King once said, "we are tied together in a single garment of destiny, caught in an inescapable network of mutuality." The Project started as a project, with one real vision in mind. We didn't know where we were yet going, or to what we were called. But we believed that Love was an actionable thing. And so we asked a basic question. Can we love one another, with no-strings attached...and can Love be enough? Well this project has become a movement, become what we always knew to be true; no longer a project, but a reality. Compassion changes everything...and Love Wins.

Our Mission

The Jonah Project is a 501(c)3 non-profit organization.

The Jonah Project exists to serve at-risk youth and trafficking victims through Rescue/Relocation, Shelter, & Advocacy.

We are a Christian ministry; which means that we center our values on who we believe Jesus to be, and who we are in Him. Ultimately, whether through physical, emotional, or spiritual nourishment we want to feed a child rather than a program. And we believe in building real, authentic, relationships while offering leverage-free resources. Which means our assistance isn't based on others professing a certain type of faith. Or sexual orientation. Or being anything other than in need. We believe by openly expressing our faith and mission, that others can feel free to openly express who they are. In that way, we can build real, authentic relationships based on loving one another.

The Jonah Project   RESCUE LINE: 509-655-7886   www.jonahproject.org

4.2-WHAT WE DO

The 5 "R's"

1. **REACH OUT**: We reach out to the community by creating awareness through education, training, and pushing for changes in the way our city serves at-risk youth and survivors of human trafficking. We also relationally engage with churches, schools, nonprofits, government agencies, and other community organizations.

2. **RESCUE**: As well as taking referrals from other organizations, we maintain a 24/7 Rescue Line for trafficking victims who want out, including sending out a team of trained individuals to safely extract victims who may lack the freedom to leave of their own free will.

3. **RELOCATION**: From the use of designated host homes to an "underground railroad" network, we relocate trafficking victims when their safety necessitates a significant geographical change.

4. **REST**: We maintain a network of volunteer host home families as well as safe homes where trafficking victims can find a safe, healing environment to rest (often receiving their first full night of sleep in a long while), and begin the process of rebuilding their lives.

5. **RESOURCES**: During their stay, residents are provided with shelter, food, and clothing free of charge. They are also paired with an advocate to walk 1:1 with them through the rebuilding process, help them to explore choices, and serve as a bridge to connect them with other area resources available to them such as medical care, mental health services, public transportation, education, and employment opportunities. When The Jonah Project is unable to provide an adequate level of care in terms of placement or counseling, we will advocate on their behalf for the best solution to meet their needs.

The Jonah Project   RESCUE LINE: 509-655-7886   www.jonahproject.org

5-GUIDING PRINCIPLE: TRANPSARENT AFTERCARE

UNDERSTANDING TRAFFICKING VICTIMS

Why we developed a freedom-based, relationship-centered, transparent after-care model.

1. **MULTIPLE TRAUMAS**: Often, the circumstances which led to someone being trafficked were traumatic in and of themselves (poverty, neglect, homelessness). Thus, rather than a single trauma, many trafficking victims suffer from multiple abuse trauma. This means that there may also be several active coping mechanisms in place.

2. **FEAR & DISTRUST**: At times, victims of trafficking have a fear or distrust of the government and police because they fear being deported, or because they experienced corruption and abuse from law enforcement in their country of origin. In other cases, their lives and the lives of their families may be at great risk if they attempt to escape their servitude or initiate criminal investigations against their captors. Then of course there is the fear generated by the abuse. Victims will appear hyper-vigilant and/or be "triggered" into episodes of panic by various means. Finally, they may simply not see themselves as they type of people who relay on shelters or assistance.

3. **DISASSOCIATION & DETACHMENT**: Some victims have cried out every single night for years to be rescued. They may believe no one cares, or even that they are being punished for running away or being bad. Over time, they may come to believe that this is simply "their life," forgetting that they once had dreams and aspirations that didn't include being forced to have sex. Day after day they fall deeper and deeper into a "walking death." Slowly and surely their minds and hearts withdraw from the desire to engage in any kind of healthy relationship—if they even believe that it is still an available option. They begin to detach and disassociate with the living world around them, like a 24/7 sleepwalk, which is something often witnessed during the intake process and 72 hour evaluation.

4. **ADDICTIONS**: Whether to dull the pain, due to cultural norms, or simply because they were forced to by their trafficker, the vast majority of trafficking victims will require drug counseling or rehabilitation at some point. Addictions are common as a result of coping strategies or even by design of the trafficker who uses the addiction and resulting debt as leverage and control over the victim. Alcohol is common but hard drugs compose some of the biggest obstacles that victims—and those who attempt to help them—will face.

5. **The Critical Figure**: As a coping or survival skill, victims of trafficking may have developed loyalties, attachments, and positive feelings towards their trafficker. They may even try to protect them from authorities.

| The Jonah Project | RESCUE LINE: 509-655-7886 | www.jonahproject.org |

5-GUIDING PRINCIPLE: TRANPSARENT AFTERCARE

PRINCIPLES OF TRANSPARENT AFTER CARE

Each resident will have different needs based on their age and the particulars of their situation; as a result, their care plan needs to be adjusted based on their individual need or else resources will be wasted and victims will be more likely to return to the streets or relapse into addictions. That being said, there are a few core principles woven through The Jonah Project's relationship-based approach to treating trafficking survivors:

1. **TRANSPARENCY**: We will be OPEN and HONEST in the way we associate with and interact with trafficking survivors and volunteers. If we believe that love wins, we have nothing to hide in our process and we can be a model for other agencies to show them that such transparency works. In addition, one of the main responsibilities of advocates will be to follow up and ensure that other Resource Providers are also delivering what they have promised to our residents.

2. **CONFIDENTIALITY**: All staff members who have contact with a trafficking survivor, including interpreters and advocates, will understand the importance of and practice confidentiality for their safety.

3. **FAITH & FREEDOM**: Choice and freedom are not things trafficking victims are familiar with, so we will—with great patience—provide a safe and secure structure for this process to play out over time. We will always ensure advocates are available to help them navigate making free choices about their own care. Although we do require residents to stay engaged (since their progress depends on it), whenever possible we want the resident to be empowered to choose, even if it means to decline our care. The only exception would be care that is medically prescribed or a government enforced requirement. In addition, while we are a Christian, faith-based organization, we will not force our faith on residents, make it a requirement to receive our services, nor discriminate against those of other religious or non-religious backgrounds. Finally, we will not use guilt or shame as tools of control in survivors struggle for freedom or fight against addictions.

4. **REPLACING THE CRITICAL FIGURE**: The Jonah Project is aware of the critical figure dynamic with survivors of trafficking and of the need to function as a replacement for toxic critical figures in their lives. With integrity, patience, love, and a relationship-based (as opposed to a program-based) approach, we will endeavor to model new, appropriate critical figures in their lives.

The Jonah Project   RESCUE LINE: 509-655-7886   www.jonahproject.org

6-RESOURCE <=> RESIDENT SPHERE OF INFLUENCE

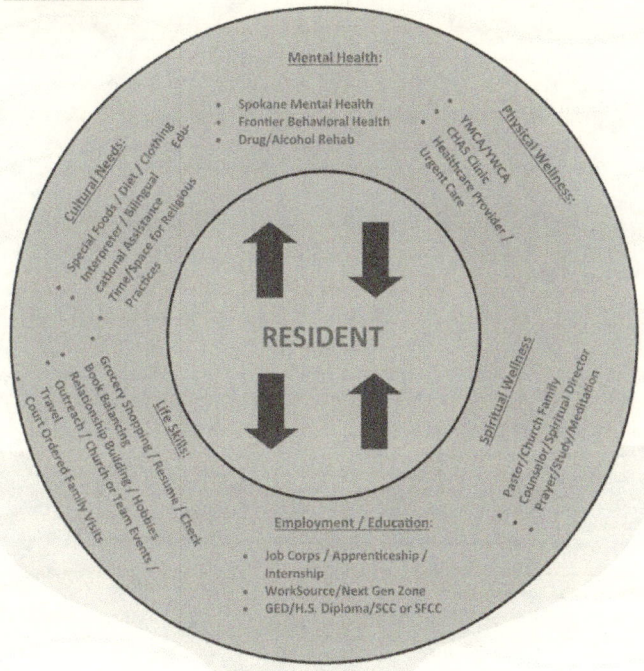

7-INTERVIEW & ASSESSMENT INFO AND CHECKLIST

SETTING UP THE INTERVIEW
(Data from the United States Office of Justice Programs)

The setting in which an interview takes place can be as important as the questions that are asked. Trafficking victims have often been held in servitude through threats of harm and fear of their arrest or deportation by police and immigration authorities. It is crucial to establish a safe space to help victims feel more comfortable and protected. To help allay victims' fears from the onset of an interview, the following techniques have proven effective:

- Hold the interview in a non-threatening and comfortable location.
- Provide the victim with food, drink, and incidentals including tissues, regular breaks, and a place where the victim can gain their composure if the interview causes distress.
- Consider dressing in casual clothing, especially when visiting agricultural labor camps to reach out to potential victims. Dressing in uniforms and other formal attire may create fears that interviewers are from immigration or other enforcement agencies.
- Be honest at the beginning about the purpose and duration of the screening. Describe the victim's rights, the interview process, and the roles of everyone involved.
- Employ competent, trustworthy interpreters if the victim's first language is not English. Competent interpreters ask questions using the same wording as the screener and answer as fully as the victim. The victim must be assured of confidentiality.
- Be aware of gender issues and ask victims if they would be more comfortable being interviewed by someone of the same gender.

The Jonah Project   RESCUE LINE: 509-655-7886   www.jonahproject.org

7-INTERVIEW & ASSESSMENT INFO AND CHECKLIST

DEVELOPING TRUST / DEMONSTRATING RESPECT DURING INTERVIEWS:

Trafficking victims need to feel safe with the interviewer before they divulge experiences that may revive fears and feelings of distress, or place themselves or their families in further jeopardy. Some service providers may judge that it is in the victim's interest to have a general conversation first and return to the screening questions at a second meeting. When the victim is ready to answer the victim identification questions, interviewers may wish to keep the following techniques in mind:

- *Be patient, caring, and sensitive to the victim's fears of retribution and the possible consequences of being identified as a victim or a party to trafficking crimes. Many victims are not familiar with laws and victim protections regarding trafficking.*

- *Be careful not to imply that a victim was responsible for their own abuse and exploitation or for the inability to leave a trafficking situation. Reassure them that others have been in similar situations and, as victims of a crime, they are not to blame.*

- *Take the time necessary to allow victims to recount the story, which may mean holding several meetings. Allow the victim to direct the interview and to tell their story in their own words. They should also feel free to stop the interview at any point if they experience distress. Take as many breaks as needed and ask for assistance from the JP Director if you need help!*

- *Be respectful of the victim's cultural background including social etiquette, religious observances, societal status, ethnic community ties, customs of clothing, and attitudes towards sex.*

- *Be aware that cultural differences may make some topics such as sex and mental health uncomfortable to discuss. Some messages to convey include: "We are here to help you;" "You can trust me;" "Your safety is our first priority;" and "You have a right to live without being abused."*

The Jonah Project RESCUE LINE: 509-655-7886 www.jonahproject.org

7-INTERVIEW & ASSESSMENT INFO AND CHECKLIST

UNDERSTANDING THE EFFECTS OF TRAUMA & VICTIMIZATION:

Trafficking victims have often endured profound physical and psychological injuries that may impede the efforts of attorneys and other service providers to interview them and develop strong working relationships. Minimization, denial, and memory loss—which are symptoms of psychological trauma—can make it extremely difficult to elicit consistent information. Below are important points regarding trauma and victimization to keep in mind:

- *Express Sorrow for what has happened to them, but do not appear to be judgmental or shocked by the details they reveal.*
- *Ask only basic questions about mental health unless you are trained as a mental health professional. A few straightforward, non–intrusive questions asked in a kind manner can convey a caring attitude and help the screener and the victim decide if a referral to a mental health professional is desirable or necessary.*
- *Be understanding when victims do not wish to repeat the details of the crime. Keep in mind that recounting stories many times for various people (social service agencies, lawyers, law enforcement, and so forth) may cause victims to re-experience trauma. Try to minimize the potential for re-traumatization when possible.*

7-INTERVIEW & ASSESSMENT INFO AND CHECKLIST

SPECIFIC FOR UNDER 18:

When Children/youth (<18 years) are involved, force, deception, or other means need not be present. Commercial sexual exploitation of children (CSEC) is closely related to sex trafficking and involves "crimes of a sexual nature committed against juvenile victims for financial or other economic reasons." These crimes include trafficking for sexual purposes, prostitution, sex tourism, mail-order bride trade, early marriage, pornography, stripping, and preforming in sexual venues such as peep shows or clubs." Many also include "survival sex" in this definition (exchange of sexual activity for basic necessities such as shelter, food, or money), a practice commonly seen among homeless / runaway youth. When CSEC involves US Citizens of legal residents victimized on US territory, this is termed domestic minor sex trafficking (American Academy of Pediatrics).

Once a victim of trafficking is identified, the advocate clinician and client 2will need to put together a plan of care. The health care provider should be aware of the following:

1. The provider cannot force the victim to report the crime
2. The victim and/or victim's family may be at risk for immense harm if she/he reports the crime.
3. If the victim is a minor, the provider is under legal obligation to phone child protective services.

The Jonah Project   RESCUE LINE: 509-655-7886   www.jonahproject.org

7-INTERVIEW & ASSESSMENT INFO AND CHECKLIST

HEALTH:

The health problems seen in victims of trafficking are largely a result of several factors: deprivation of food and sleep, extreme stress, hazards of travel, violence (physical and sexual), and hazardous work. Because most victims do not have timely access to health care, by the time they reach a clinician it is likely that health problems are well advanced. These women are at a high risk for acquiring multiple sexually transmitted infections and the results of multiple forced and unsafe abortions. Physical abuse and torture often occur, which can result in broken bones, contusions, dental problems (e.g., loss of teeth), and/or cigarette burns. Psychological violence results in high rates of post traumatic stress disorder, depression, suicidal ideation, and drug addiction. When providers were asked in one study about their experiences working with victims of trafficking, they reported that these victims are less stable, more isolated, and have higher levels of fear, more severe trauma, and greater mental health needs than other victims of crime. One trafficking victim can take the same amount of the provider's time as 20 domestic violence victims.

- Anxiety
- Chronic pain
- Cigarette burns
- Complications from unsafe abortion
- Contusions
- Depression
- Fractures
- Gastrointestinal problems

- Headaches
- Oral health problems
- Pelvic pain
- Post Traumatic Stress Disorder
- Sexually transmitted infections
- Suicidal ideation
- Unhealthy weight loss
- Unwanted pregnancy

Common problems seen in victims of trafficking (US National Library of Medicine):

14-ASSESSMENT TEAM GOALS

(Facilitators/Advocates & House Leaders)

24 Hours

1. Emergency Medical Care
2. Bedding
3. Dietary Restrictions
4. Personal Care Items
5. Interpreter Needs
6. Clothing
7. Introduction to House Leader(s)
8. Review/Discuss House "Safety Plan"

72 Hours

1. Complete Initial Interview
2. Schedule Medical Appointment (HIV/TB)

Day 20+

1. Facilitate Access to Counseling / Mental Health Resources
2. Orientation to Neighborhood & Public Transit
3. EBT Application; I.D. & Personal Documents Assistance
4. House Meeting / Church Gathering
5. Assign Advocate

The Jonah Project   RESCUE LINE: 509-655-7886   www.jonahproject.org

15-VOLUNTEER DO'S & DON'TS

REMEMBER!

1. Due to power & control dynamics, many teens and trauma victims we meet may not identify as victims.

2. Victims in this traumatic situation have typically been conditioned by their trafficker not to trust law enforcement or social service providers.

3. Canned stories are common, and the true story may not emerge until trust has been built with the potential victim after multiple meetings.

4. Each potential victim is going to tell his/her story differently; no individual will present all of the details of his/her situation in a neat, perfectly linear package.

5. Be aware of power & control dynamics when a third party (such as a friend, family member, or other "interested" party) is accompanying or interpreting for a potential victim. If possible, speak to the potential victim one-on-one in a safe, public space and/or secure an outside interpreter.

DO!

1. Prioritize the victim's confidentiality.
2. Remain flexible as much as possible.
3. Speak in straightforward language.
4. Document your conversation.
5. Prioritize your own safety as well.

DON'T!

1. Pressure the victim to engage law enforcement.
2. Use leverage, power, or arguments to obtain facts.
3. Rush your interview.

The Jonah Project   RESCUE LINE: 509-655-7886   www.jonahproject.org

Made in the USA
Coppell, TX
23 February 2026

72230345R00080